REFLECTIONS
FROM A
NARROWBOAT

To Kathy
x Alice x

BY
ALICE WHITE

Reflections from a Narrowboat
By Alice White

ISBN: 978-1-7390972-0-2

Published by Gossage Vears Publications, 2022

Illustrations by Charlotte Harker
Edited by Siân-Elin Flint-Freel
Book design by Tanya Bäck, www.tanyabackdesigns.com

*To my family and friends who –
without making judgements on some
of my more crazy decisions – were
always there to catch me if they
didn't work out.*

*However, I hope they'll follow my
philosophy of life and when they get
the choice to sit it out or dance –
I hope they dance.*

The Beginning

'It's better to be unhappy alone than unhappy with someone —so far.'

Marilyn Monroe

t is a couple of months before my 50th Birthday; I long to have 'someone special' to share it with at the party I have been planning for family and friends since I was 48. I know from the moment I open the door of my tiny fisherman's cottage and he bounds in barefoot like an overexcited Labrador puppy, hugging me so hard I gasp out in shock, that this man will have a profound effect on my life.

There is a split second of doubt in my mind as with a careless flourish he scatters his few possessions across the floor in the middle of my already heavily furnished tiny sitting room – a ragged well-worn black canvas camera bag and a huge and even more tattered black leather-bound art portfolio which promptly bursts open, dispersing faded pencil sketches of nudes across the floor, like a tarot card reader randomly laying out a spread. I feel slightly disorientated for a moment and then compose myself a little, catch my breath and settle on the thought of 'It will be fine. What have I got to lose?'

As it turned out, I did lose quite a lot – although mainly materialistic things, including (almost) my cottage – although overall, I recognise now I gained much more. I learned not only some of the basic skills needed to survive, but also much about my relationship with nature, people, and more importantly, myself. I believe for the first time that I am living my life authentically.

I continue to benefit from my experiences in my work and my life – as the wise philosopher Socrates said: 'The unexamined life is not worth living.' As I write this, I hope you, the reader, can gain some insights from reading it too.

This collection of stories relates some of my adventures as I recall them, drawn from blogs I wrote and sent to family and friends during the three years or so I lived on a narrowboat. Also, some reflections about many of the people and events that touched my life and some useful facts about narrowboating life if you are considering having an adventure of your own.

Some of the stories inevitably refer to time spent with the above-mentioned 'Labrador' on his boat, but mainly they are my reflections, experiences and life lessons learned on my own.

The more self-aware among you, or indeed those of you who have experienced similar difficult personal relationships, will no doubt realise from my story that I was being manipulated by this seemingly charming man who I now recognise had many narcissistic traits.

However, in the words of Carl Jung, 'The meeting of two personalities is like the contact of two chemical substances: if there is any reaction, both are transformed.'

I doubt I would have had the opportunity to savour this lifestyle had it not been for the Labrador and I now thank him for that and hope he has also benefitted from some form of transformation too.

This is the book that family and friends encouraged me to write as they enjoyed the humour I wove into the blogs I shared with them via email while I was 'away'. I'm guessing few of them recognised at the time what I also learned much later during my psychotherapy training and personal therapy experiences, that this was the humour I had long learned to employ to hide my insecurities, unhappiness and fears about my often perceived inevitable abandonment in relationships. Following my official diagnosis of dyslexia during these invaluable training years, along with the realisation I had a fair smattering of a Schizoid personality process, humour has also often been my 'go to' creative defence – I found amusing others was a great distraction to hide my fears of not fitting in.

This story is just the beginning of my emerging self-awareness through what turned out to be an extraordinary and reflective journey experienced on some of the canals of England and beyond.

The Invitation

'I want to know if
you will risk looking
like a fool for love,
for your dream, for the
adventure of being alive...
It doesn't interest me if
the story you are telling
me is true.'

Oriah Mountain Dreamer

We met on an online dating site. As I write these words I almost know what you are thinking – the potential risks involved in this type of meeting.

I don't really know what I was thinking. Although loneliness is a great distraction from logical thought and reinforced my belief that we were 'meant for each other'. We had so much in common – or so it seemed to me. In reality, the only thing we had in common was our star sign – our birthdays being five days apart. But he was so fascinating, charismatic and easy to talk to and seemed to understand me so well.

After talking online many times – often throughout the night – we had met in person only once, at the annual music and arts Strawberry Fair in Cambridge, where his narrowboat was moored. After this one meeting, it seemed we were hooked; it seemed like the perfect match and he was keen to meet my family and be by my side for ever. It just made sense for him to move in with me.

It was barely a year after this that he started to make it clear how much he missed his boat and his previous peripatetic lifestyle. Just the odd word here and there – the 'beauty of the canal at Cassiobury Park where it passes through a nature reserve' or 'the adventures on the Kennet and Avon stretch that links the two rivers'. I'd catch him giving a wistful gaze out to sea on one of our beach walks, followed by the awkward (for me) silences when I asked him if he was OK.

We had by then spent several pleasant carefree balmy summer weekends on his boat, moving it from Cambridge to finally moor near the Toll House Café at Cowley Peachey on the Grand Union Canal in the London borough of Hillingdon. The café was run by a particularly stressed, hard working and grumpy looking woman called Julie, who wasn't particularly welcoming towards me. The Labrador seemed to know her quite well and had been paying her to use her address for post. He inconspicuously dropped into a conversation one evening that I should do the same when we moved there.

I don't recall agreeing to move to live on his boat, although again I found myself making that decision which felt entirely autonomous. Before I knew it, I was excitedly telling everyone about our new adventure as if I'd planned it myself from the start.

REFLECTIONS:

 When you think you're in love, logical thinking goes out of the window – or in this case, the porthole.

 A good plan when making a big decision is to take a deep breath and ask yourself – 'Do I really want to do this or is it to please someone else?'

The Arrival

'You don't bring me
flowers anymore.'

Neil Diamond/Alan and Marilyn Bergman

t was the hottest day of the year – 2006 – when we again travelled to the Labrador's boat. Not just for a weekend this time, but to live on it. It was also the day that England lost to Portugal and therefore abandoned any hope of winning the World Cup.

As we drove away from my cosy fisherman's cottage home in Winterton-on-Sea, our cars packed up to the sunroof, parked cars and houses adorned with the flags of St. George to encourage the national team gradually thinned out. By the time we reached the M11, the only car with this familiar emblem was in a lay-by being attended by an AA man; the owner, dressed in his England shirt, standing forlornly by, all hopes of watching the match on TV slipping away from him. As we both hated football with a passion, we had little sympathy as we set off to our – in reality, my – new life.

Even the air conditioning in my car could not compete with the intense heat, and by the time we arrived we were exhausted, sweaty and I was becoming a little panicky.

'What had I done? Where was the nice cool shower?' The only signs of fresh water being the puddle that covered the slightly dubious stains on the well-worn and grubby carpet where the boat hatches had seemingly leaked the last time it rained!

Too tired to unpack the car, we fell into (or in my case over) the bed that we had, with much huffing and swearing, constructed with difficulty in the small, musty smelling and gloomy space that was to be my new home.

It was beginning to dawn on me that my new life was possibly going to be very different to how I had experienced it during the exciting and romantic weekends we had spent visiting his boat over the previous spring and summer. The first of these had been particularly alluring, where the Labrador had enticed me by seductively scattering daisies and other wild flowers over the bed.

This delightful memory seemed distant now as I lay on the bed of the forty-foot, rotting and uncared for narrowboat (Why had I never noticed before?) which was not necessarily designed to accommodate two people comfortably – or even uncomfortably. Why on earth did I think it would be the ideal place within which to progress a relatively new and successful relationship?

The Labrador, I have since realised, had 'come home' and no longer cared if I was happy with our living arrangement.

I was surprised how well I had slept that first night, maybe rocked to slumber by the boat's very gentle movement. We awoke to another scorching hot day and the offer of a meal that night from friends of the Labrador – a couple and their three-year-old son who lived on the boat moored opposite ours. I say 'friends' and offer a bit of an explanation, as I later discovered two things that for me contradict that term.

Firstly, that friends and neighbours are much more of a transient concept when living on a boat. I note this because unless you hold a fixed mooring (as rare as Malta winning the Eurovision Song Contest) or opt to live in a marina (which to me would feel a bit like a caravan site), no one is reliably static. I built quite a connection with the folk 'next door' on several occasions, only to wake up early the next morning to find they had moved on, with no certainty I would ever see them again. This came to feel quite destabilising for me, especially given what was to come.

I also came to realise that the Labrador's relationships with his friends – as he described them – were quite fragile. He often spoke of past friends in quite a derogatory way. Often he said they had wronged him – for me, it sounded in quite trivial ways – leading to him abruptly cutting them out of his life for ever.

Anyway, these particular 'friends' were originally from New Zealand and they spoke of their longing to return there one day. Allie was a professional cook, and the meal she made us was delicious – a fragrant curry dish with both sweet and savoury spices which left my mouth confused but satisfied. I was in awe as to how she created such amazing food in a kitchen area the size of a matchbox. I was also fascinated and a little muddled by their accents – Allie's (being a Kiwi) was even more broad and distinctive than her husband, Jack. With the strange (to me) replacement of vowels and upspeak at the end of sentences, it took me a while to work out their names were not Illie and Jeck, or for that matter, when (or even if) I was being asked a 'quistion'. We ate, plates balanced precariously on our knees, seated on Charlie's (their son) rumpled bed, squashed between him and their unruly, enormous and boisterous Great Dane which seemed to me a rather ambitious choice of dog for such a small living area. The former appeared to have an endlessly snotty nose and the latter alternated between trying to steal our food from our plates or mate with us. I was not quite sure which felt worse so I tried to focus on wondering how:

- ⚓ Allie could possibly keep her kitchen work surfaces clean amid this chaos, and
- ⚓ my normally delicate stomach would survive the night, given the potential combination of ingested salmonella and dog poo.

Obviously, I did survive that encounter and, although I don't recall directly, I was already instinctively feeling an element of uncertainty. Over the next couple of days, this uncertainty led me to wonder how I might earn a living in order to maintain some independence should this relationship with the Labrador fall apart.

I had been a district nurse most of my working life. In the ten years prior to the death of my previous partner of twenty-five years, I had worked as a Home Respite Care manager for a large charity. My partner's death after a short but traumatic illness led me to make another huge life change and I ran away in some sort of self-imposed isolation to start a 'new' life in Norfolk, leaving behind my family and friends. I had worked in Norfolk as a Hospice at Home manager. After some thought about how I might use some of these skills, I decided to look for work as a health and social care assessor and teacher in nearby Uxbridge and Hounslow.

The Labrador's background was very different to mine, born into a military family with a period spent in care due to what I understood to be his mother's mental breakdown and alcoholism, and his father's brutality. Unlike me, he had moved house many times (more than twenty) in his early life. When we first 'met' on the online dating site, his picture was nothing like he first appeared when we met in person and had clearly been taken several years before, when he was much slimmer. I always managed to justify these inconsistencies – such as his weight gain being due to his unhappiness over the cruelty and deceit his ex-wife had shown towards him. I chose not to believe why he might have tried to create a false picture of himself to 'win me over'.

Looking back, I find it strange that I didn't think it unusual that the only close friend he said he had, he spoke of with contempt, along with the many other people from his past, who he said had 'let him down', not least his daughter. He had developed a way of shutting these people out of his life and became angry and evasive if I attempted to question him about them so I always took his side and sympathised with him for his 'bad luck' in relationships.

I preferred to focus on ensuring some of the horror stories I had heard about internet dating didn't happen to me, and this seemed unlikely as he was extremely generous with the little money he had – always paying his way. I took up the grumpy-woman-at-the-cafe's offer of a postal address. It felt reassuring that family and friends would have an additional way to contact me and important as I needed to receive official letters relating to my house, car, etc.

I remained curious about the Labrador's past and therefore knowing what post he was receiving also satisfied me to some extent, although he was still quite selective in what he showed me.

He found graphic design work shortly after I invited him to move in with me to the cottage. He was very keen to show off his skills by helping me to design a new website to write my blogs and publish my photos and later – when living on his boat – to promote my self-employed business. He also showered me with gifts, including some pretty and unusual jewellery. Not expensive items as we didn't have a lot of money to spare, but clearly the styles he knew I would like or maybe what he would like for me? It was hard not to enjoy this devoted attention after a while – and he did have very good taste.

My new life felt exciting and I was beginning to enjoy the ease of access into London while living outside the hustle and bustle and so cheaply. However, it was often difficult to find a parking space near the boat and having to carry bags of shopping quite a distance along the towpath was somewhat challenging. This was all the more frustrating when I struggled to remember where we had 'parked' the boat when walking back from 'town' on a weekend trip to the Thames at Teddington Lock or the huge Tesco at Bulls Bridge in Southall, where we bought fragrant spices and exotic vegetables unavailable in the less culturally diverse places where I was used to living. I learned to make delicious authentic curries in an equally tiny kitchen area to our neighbours. I once bought a strange looking vegetable to cook for our evening meal, which resembled a large dark green chilli with a very wrinkled skin. I duly washed and peeled it and chopped the remains, putting them in the pot with everything else. It tasted really bitter and we spat it out, only to find out later from Allie that I had thrown the wrong bit away and should have soaked the skin in salt water and served it as a separate vegetable.

One advantage of travelling by boat was the ability to get right into the heart of the city and not have to worry about parking or battling with the crowded tube trains. This was how we arrived at Notting Hill Carnival on another brilliantly hazy, sunny August weekend. This magnificent colourful event was buzzing with its processions, steel bands, calypso music and people of all cultures dancing along the streets lined with food stalls. Smoke curling from the jerk chicken pits was the first smell to hit the senses, followed by a concoction of other delectably authentic Caribbean delicacies. If your taste buds were not assaulted enough by the curried goat or Ackee and Saltfish, you could always wash it down with a spicy rum cocktail and not worry about drink driving.

Travelling to the carnival was my first big adventure, driving his boat cautiously through the pitch-black night – no street lamps on the canal – feeling secure in the knowledge he was down below doing whatever he was doing on his laptop and would be there to take over if I needed him to. I didn't find out (or maybe I didn't want to know) what he was doing 'down below' until much later in our relationship, when I realised there were probably several other women he was still in touch with from his online dating days.

As we approached the bridge at Ladbroke Grove, boats that had already arrived were two or three deep vying for the best mooring to attend this spectacular annual event. The air was thick with the smell of cannabis hanging as a cloud just above the crowded water. I got very used to this aroma and although I didn't smoke as much or as often as the Labrador – he did everything to excess and I instinctively felt the need to maintain control when I was around him – I have always enjoyed that fragrant sweetness and relaxing effect. I popped my head inside and asked the Labrador to take care of the mooring. I'd never attempted to 'double or triple park' before. This was not in my skill set.

Of the many skills I acquired during my first few months on the water, I had come to realise and inwardly enjoy the fact that I was becoming a pretty good photographer – although I didn't have the confidence to boast about this to the Labrador. He had initially encouraged me to buy my first 'proper' camera but did not like me being better than him at anything. He patiently tried to teach me the technical details without success. My dyslexic brain could never cope with fractions and to this day I don't understand what terms such as 'depth of field' and 'focal point' mean. However, I happily snapped away, unconsciously capturing some great shots, even without acquiring these skills, and he had to grudgingly – although only once – admit: "You have a good eye for composition." I was reluctant to dwell on the glow I felt when he said this, knowing he wouldn't like me to show too much confidence in my newly acquired skill.

The next day, near noon, people started to emerge sleepily from their boats and make their way to find a good viewing spot in the street. As the procession approached, we lay on the ground – our cameras pointing hopefully upwards – or raced up and down the road of the magnificently colourful event, competing to get the clever angle shot of the carnival. It was on this day that I realised being better than him at anything was an unwritten rule that was not allowed. He showed his displeasure by going silent and not responding to my attempts to retrospectively admire his work. As often happened on these occasions, I attempted to dismiss my worries about him seemingly to be angry with me and continued to tread carefully around him, preferring to believe in the image he portrayed to the world – the sensitive, artistic, misunderstood character – as this appealed to me greatly.

One Monday, after one of these weekend trips, I recall becoming disorientated (all the towpaths looked the same to me) when trying to find where his boat was moored and walked for what seemed like miles alone with bags of shopping, along the towpath in the wrong direction. I felt completely adrift and scared myself wondering what I would do if I never found my way home. The Labrador would often move his boat to a different mooring spot without forewarning me – a sign of his gaslighting? - and ignore me, shutting me out of his consciousness for days. When I complained, he would again talk to me as though I was a child, making light of my concerns, which left me feeling foolish.

He was always happy and confident to move around – I assumed due to his disrupted childhood – and had little understanding or concerns for my fears, which to me were familiar and real feelings of abandonment triggered by often getting lost as a child. On at least one occasion I remember it being hours before my mother came to look for me. This made more sense when I was a little older and she told me on many occasions she didn't really want me as a baby and only had me to please my dad. At the times when I was lost I could never understand the anger she expressed when she 'found' me – was she not as relieved as me to be reunited?

Still, my long-practised resilience meant the positives of this life – for the time being anyway – outweighed the negatives. However, a little niggle in the very back of my mind was wondering if sharing a boat, really only meant for one and already adding tensions to our disintegrating relationship, was a good idea.

REFLECTIONS:

 You have the right to ask questions if you don't know much about someone with whom you are considering starting a relationship.

 When people get angry with you it's usually more about them than you.

 It is said people often instinctively choose a partner who is like their parent – ironically, often a parent who they historically longed to escape from.

 It's OK to own what you are good at, to feel proud of yourself, and talk about it.

I Think I Want To
Go Home—
Do I?

'Your old home town's
so far away, but inside
your head there's a
record that's playing a
song called "Hold On".'

Tom Waits

However, in contrast with the quote at the beginning of this chapter, I held in mind the even more powerful voice of my long deceased mother who, on the few occasions I dared to ask her for help when I'd made an impulsive decision, seemed to take delight in saying rather cruelly, "You've made your bed, now lie on it!" My bed felt well and truly made.

Although I had not sold my house in Norfolk – having wisely at the time rented it out – this led me to realise I had made another unwise choice around men.

Not wanting to spend the additional money to rent through a letting agent, I rather smartly (I thought) wrote my own tenancy agreement for a rather nice man who had shown me two references – one being from his current employer.

After three months of prompt payment of rent, the payments suddenly stopped.

I called him.

He apologised.

I called again.

He apologised again, blaming his bank and offering to investigate – still no rent appeared.

I called my neighbour in Norfolk, who said my tenant had looked perfectly well when she saw him each day sitting outside the local pub with a beer and a newspaper and that he never appeared to go to work.

I called him again – tentatively asking if he still had a job and offering to help out if he was in trouble. He said all was fine and he would call his bank again to see what they had done wrong.

Still no rent appeared.

I began the lengthy process of eviction – or so I thought, not appreciating at the time that nothing was happening solicitor-wise, and what happened next afforded me some breathing space. I put my house worries in that filing cabinet in the back of my mind where all the bad things are stored.

So I couldn't go back and I was wondering if I could go forward with the Labrador and his long, cold silences, a shower that alternated between emitting little more than a dribble of either scalding hot or freezing cold water, and the disgusting prospect of emptying not one but two people's excrement into a stinking pit every few days.

Three months into this new life, it became obvious that the two of us in a confined space, on HIS boat, next to HIS acquaintances, was not going to pan out. He was very adept at triggering my poor self-esteem, self-doubt and guilty feelings when (in his eyes) I was being critical towards him and what he clearly saw as his 'perfect' boat.

And then I had another of my brilliant ideas…

REFLECTIONS:

 I have the right to make decisions based on any reason I choose, and the right to change my mind at any time.

 If someone tries to control you, it doesn't mean they care about you.

 Take legal advice when your home depends on it – it will probably save you as much as it costs, if only in stress and anxiety.

Branching Out

'I was much too far out
all my life, and not
waving but drowning.'

Stevie Smith

Not being one to hesitate when I get an idea, especially a big and potentially life-changing one, I tend to make decisions very quickly – a controversial trait I have gifted to my youngest daughter.

The decision to buy a boat of my own was one of these swift decisions that first occurred to me not long after we had arrived in Cowley. On this occasion, it served me well. In the short term particularly, when I needed to gain some space to escape temporarily from my fast becoming difficult relationship with the Labrador, and in the longer term…well, more about that later.

Excited to be collecting my new purchase, a tiny 32-foot narrowboat from Whilton Marina, where it was moored for sale, I was very keen to prove my newly acquired but limited boating skills. I was impatient when going through the paperwork and technical instructions and eager to escape the (in my opinion) unnecessary rules and restrictions of the Marina manager. Never being one to be able to concentrate on following verbal instructions

(I now attribute this to a feature of my dyslexia, diagnosed much later in my life), I automatically dismissed much of what was being said by the manager, who seemed a bit of a health and safety fanatic to me. I mean, what did they know about my new home? How hard could it be?

Fortunately (or maybe unfortunately at this time), I was unaware of the frightening statistics from the National Water Safety Forum,[1] showing the numbers of people who die from 'water related incidents' each year.

At thirty-two feet in length, my new boat was probably the smallest a narrowboat gets. The Marina manager and the Labrador agreed that it would be an appropriate and manageable size 'for a woman to handle'. Unusually for me – probably in my eagerness to complete my purchase – I hid my disapproval at this sexist comment and vowed from then on to refer to my boat as 'he' as a passive rebellion to the 'she' gender pronoun usually attributed to boats and cars by men.

However, I couldn't hide the fact that I did find 'him' cute, with his tiny pot-bellied wood burning stove surrounded by deep blue vintage tiles. The little portholes were big enough to be my windows looking out on the water and surrounding countryside but small enough to protect my privacy. The rustic pine wood panelling adorned with polished brass badges told the story of journeys of his past owners.

I discovered that my boat was originally built in 1970 by Eric Wood from a recycled gas holder and had maintained the original Lister engine, which always

---

1 http://www.nationalwatersafety.org.uk/

sounded to me like a quieter version of the reassuring gentle 'chug chug pop' of the old steam trains. When sold in 1990, his name was changed from Credalwood to Argy Bargy. The full story of his whereabouts until my purchase is not recorded, although I believe the name change was driven by the fact that the previous owners had got divorced. Of course, I was way too excited to imagine this could possibly be a bad omen of any sort.

Exams and tests of any nature have always been a challenge to me and even to this day fill me with some dread. I saw this challenge of mastering my new purchase in a similar light to a test – and given the perceived low expectations of the Labrador and the Marina manager in my abilities, one I was determined to pass.

I recall at a very early age – around five years old I think – one minute I was enjoying dancing daintily around in a circle as a flower girl in a ballet lesson and the next crying to my mum that I never wanted to go back. She did nothing either to offer an explanation or indeed reassure me when I tried through my tears to tell her I had overheard the dance teacher saying we were to take an exam the following week. In my child's mind, I had assumed it was some sort of medical examination and my experiences of these were – even at my young age – not good. Having already spent two spells in hospital by then, I was taking no chances of what in my naïve imagination would mean being prodded, injected and abandoned again. At that time, there were still restricted visiting times, even for small children. The memory of gazing out of the window from my uncomfortably hard hospital bed with its cold and crisp sheets to see my parents disappearing around the corner – not knowing when or even if they would return – still leaves me in fear. So reluctantly, I had to give up my dreams of floating around in my longed for pink tutu (the prize that was awarded only after taking the dreaded exam).

I was – as I'm sure you are beginning to realise – an anxious child who mainly had to seek her own reassurances as no one asked me why I was so afraid or offered me any sense of security.

By the time I was ten-and-a-half, I had developed more resilience and my anxiety – although still very much present in the physical form of nausea and much actual vomiting – was channelled into a sort of dogged determination. No-one was going to tell me I couldn't do something.

The very scary headmaster at my junior school – the one who took over from the retired gentle paternal one – was a giant brute of a Yorkshireman with extremely big hands. These he used (with some relish, I think) either to pull me out in front of the class if I couldn't answer a maths question or on occasions to smack my bottom – just because he was a bully. I wasn't good with numbers – I now know due to my dyslexia – and the shame and fear of these regular humiliating and painful occurrences has stayed with me to this day, particularly emerging when faced with a simple number challenge such as adding up a restaurant bill. (Even when using a calculator, I get confused.) I overheard him telling my parents that I would never pass my eleven-plus exam. Something must have stirred in me, because although I had to leave the school hall to vomit at the first attempt, I went back and passed the exam and obtained a place at grammar school. Although he was a bully, I often wondered if he may have been aware of the one thing that would motivate me to succeed – telling me I couldn't do something.

Therefore, years later, on passing my driving test on

my first attempt, I was surprised and delighted with what I saw as another of the few real achievements in my life so far where I had managed to overcome my fears. Still glowing from this thrill, a few days later I had set off on the first lone (minus relieved instructor and 'L' plates) car journey. Fifteen minutes later, I had written off my now ex-husband's brand new car by wrapping it around a lamp post that unknowingly jumped into my path.

So now, all those years later and still not normally a confident driver (having held the belief that 'pride comes before a fall'), in my excited state, my superficial sense of self-assurance, defiance and determination took over.

Undeterred and with the previous disastrous driving experiences far from my mind, I majestically took the tiller for my maiden voyage which almost turned into my swan song.

As a proud new narrowboat owner with nil experience, I sailed away with this air of confidence from Whilton Marina, completely unaware I was shortly to find out how wilful my new charge would turn out to be. After all, narrowboating is not an extreme sport, so what could possibly go wrong? Anyone can drive a narrowboat, surely? There were only around eighty miles and sixty-three locks, and all in chilly November when there is little more than eight hours of daylight within which to negotiate them.

I thought at first people moored on the other boats in the marina were just waving me off, but on reflection, their gesticulations could have been rather ruder gestures, or even warnings of some sort. Maybe it was a type of special boater's wave that I was yet to learn, a bit like semaphore. I tried to recall what I could of this communication method from my brief time as a girl guide and then got bored with the idea, abandoning it to concentrate on getting up to what appeared to be (disappointingly) my new toy's top speed of around three miles per hour. At the same time, I was with some measure of success avoiding scraping against the many other boats moored in the marina. I was beginning to relax into the task a little and felt proud to be managing this new experience with my new charge so competently.

There are, in fact, very few technical points to know about driving a narrowboat and these are some it is important to consider:

1. Line yourself up for each manoeuvre as early as possible. If in doubt, slow down.
2. Sounding your horn is not rude. Use it to warn boats of your approach to blind corners and on difficult or narrow sections.
3. A 20-tonne boat at 3mph takes a lot of stopping, particularly when equipped with a single propeller. So, it is important to take it easy, approach bends with care and be aware that your steerage is likely to become quite wayward.
4. It is often best to use quite short bursts of throttle interspersed with the odd forward correction to help retain your line.
5. As you swing the nose to the left, the aft end will swing to the right to more or less the same degree – so think about your stern, watch your speed and give yourself enough time and water to make corrections.
6. Plan ahead. If you don't, you can find yourself running out of options and it all gets a little out of control.

So, with no consideration or knowledge of any of these nuggets of information, it slowly began to dawn on me that one of my boat's annoying little quirks was to pull to the right. What I didn't allow for was the time it would take me to correct this while unsticking the very sticky throttle in order for me to slow him down, at the same time trying to get the gear thingy into neutral or reverse as required.

This challenging manoeuvre, I soon found, requires a fair degree of both good coordination and concentration – unluckily two of my less well-developed traits and sometimes leads to my confusion between left and right movements on the tiller. All of this was difficult enough, but in addition, I was tired, having been awake for most of the previous night with the excitement and anticipation of collecting my boat.

It is often said that you see your life pass before your eyes in a near-death experience. For me, however, time seemed to stand still as the overhanging branch of the tree hurtled towards my head at an incredible speed. In what must have been only the few seconds it took to enter the murky depths of the Grand Union Canal and the realisation that my feet were well and truly stuck in the deep mud at the bottom, a multitude of thoughts entered and left my confused brain.

- ⚓ How warm the water is for the time of year.
- ⚓ How dark it is down here.
- ⚓ Is this what quicksand feels like?
- ⚓ How much water do I need to swallow before I catch Weil's Disease?[2]
- ⚓ Will the water turn red like in the film *Jaws* if I get my leg caught in the propeller that is still whizzing round?

2 Weil's disease is a bacterial infection carried by animals, most commonly rats and cattle. It can be caught by humans, most commonly through contaminated fresh water.

When I eventually emerged to the surface, gasping for breath, had anyone been around, I liked to imagine I looked a bit like they do in synchronised swimming, graceful and elegant. To be fair, I probably displayed more of a look of horror and surprise. I still had my specs on – both pairs, with readers on my head – clearly neither had aided me to spot the offending overhanging branch that was about to attack me. I was so relieved as things could have been a lot worse if my survival instinct hadn't surfaced and I had not managed to keep my legs well away from the propeller.

Fortunately, I escaped my ordeal with a bruise the size and shape of the map of Wales on my bum and left hip from hitting the edge of the boat as I fell, and a small graze on my hand. My mobile phone was still in my pocket and amazingly still worked, although all my contact numbers were lost to the fishes.

Thankfully, the Labrador (who didn't seem particularly pleased to see me emerge) tore himself away from his laptop and took over the driving at this stage. Meanwhile, I changed into my only other set of dry clothes and looked up the symptoms of the previously mentioned Weil's Disease on the internet in preparation so I would know what to expect, should I develop it at a later stage from all the water I had swallowed.

The main concern from a practical point of view was that in my dramatic exit from my boat I had somehow managed to bend the tiller into a rather strange angle. The problem was that if the tiller snapped, we would be stranded. The only option was to repair it temporarily to get us home where we would need to have another one made. To be fair, the Labrador did a great job of this with some wire and gaffer tape we found in the well deck locker and dismissed (quite patiently, I thought, in the circumstances) my suggestion that we could 'just go to a boat shop and collect a new one.' Apparently, they are made to measure.

We were way behind schedule to get back to our mooring space in time for work and we cruised for seven hours solidly to try to make up time. We moored up for the night and rose early the next morning to find we were in a small village, the nearest town being Stony Stratford. We set off to try to find a welder. Not an easy task, as it seemed that all the welders in the area that day were in bed following some sort of welding convention the night before which involved much merriment and heavy drinking. They would not be getting up until Monday morning, and even then, probably not to repair a bit of metal pipe from some silly woman's boat.

There was, however, hope on the horizon. Two minutes before closing, we arrived at the Motorist Centre in Stony Stratford and a very nice man only scratched his head for a mere moment (as only mechanics can) and then, without so much as a comment about women drivers, adeptly welded the tiller in minutes.

The other thing I lost temporarily was my dignity, although I did gain something much more important on that fateful day – a real respect for the possible dangers of narrowboating. That trip has stood me in good stead ever since.

Reflections:

 RTFH – Read the fu%*ing handbook! There is one available for almost every technical operation in life – don't be too proud to read it or at least listen to someone who has.

 It's OK to make mistakes (not fatal ones), to not be perfect and to forgive yourself.

 It's near impossible to get clothes dry without the luxury of radiators, a clothesline or a tumble dryer – in these circumstances, always have a spare set.

 Dyslexia is real and takes many forms – it's not just about reading and writing.

 There is a time and place to be proud of your achievements and there's always something new to learn to avoid reckless accidents.

What's In
A Name?

'I knew who I was this morning, but I've changed a few times since then.'

Lewis Carroll (Alice's Adventures in Wonderland)

When I first bought my small narrowboat, I never imagined I would be living on it without the Labrador as my partner, close neighbour and practical support. However, circumstances led me to that lone journey, and I came to realise eventually (as you will hear) I was all the happier for it. When I say alone, of course, I forget to mention my cantankerous ginger tomcat, Mellors – much more about him later too.

As the name of my boat suggested, many arguments occurred onboard, leading eventually to my 'aloneness' with Argy, Mellors and me battling it out and fighting to survive.

It's barely noticeable how you gradually lose a sense of your identity when living with a narcissist. I realised how important mine was, especially when I had surrendered my name.

The Labrador had taken to calling me 'Tillie'. I can't quite recall when or why this baptism took place; probably following a few glasses of Shiraz and one of our late night in-depth conversations. As often was the case, I discovered these conversations with the Labrador that began as fun, fairly swiftly turned to his displays of cold rejection. When I responded with, "I'll call you Billy" – what I saw as a reciprocal term of endearment – was not well received. I'm imagining due to the implication of 'Silly Billy'– '…a type of clown common at fairs in England during the 19th century.' One thing I found the Labrador couldn't tolerate was to appear foolish.

Although I had several thoughts about changing the name of my boat – being vaguely concerned that the previous owners had been divorced – I was not brave enough (or for that matter, could afford) to tempt fate by going against some boating superstitions.

The cost of renaming a boat is not small, nor reduced by following a boating tradition that dictates a boat has to come out of the water to be renamed, otherwise you bring all sorts of bad luck upon yourself.

Furthermore, instinct told me, now I had some degree of independence, I did not want to return to stay on the Labrador's boat while this process took place. Also, I have seen many a 'botched' job in boat painting and a good craftsman and artist is hard to find.

Irritating as it was at times, passers-by on the towpath seemed to have no qualms about loudly expressing their amusement on the name of my home. I would also frequently be shaken by what felt like an earthquake, as Argy rocked and rolled, disturbed by groups of over-zealous holiday boaters, dressed as pirates, fuelled by wine or Special Brew, and exceeding the regulatory speed of 4 mph – hardcore boaters would never do that – as they whooped with delight.

"Ooh a having a bit of argy bargy in there?"

However, my boat kept his name and I, for some time after, kept Tillie as mine, believing I needed to do this to keep the Labrador happy. That is, until later in my life when I found my own true authentic identity, realising that is nothing to do with an actual name.

REFLECTIONS:

 I can be happy with who I am and have the right to choose my own name.

 Sometimes it is what is not said that holds more meaning.

 I have the right to my own personal space and time needs.

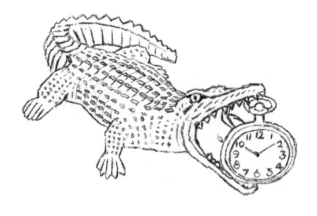

Time To Live

'Forget them, Wendy.
Forget them all.
Come with me where
you'll never, never have
to worry about grown up
things again.'

Peter Pan

'Never is an awfully
long time.'

Wendy

J.M. Barrie (Peter Pan)

Time was passing and I was struggling to remember a time when it seemed important to wear a watch to keep track of it.

One of the first things I did when we arrived at Cowley was to sit at the bow (pointy end) of the boat in the well deck (sunken area) with a large glass of Shiraz and go through my work diary. One by one, with a huge flourish, I crossed out all the pre-planned work meetings I would no longer be attending now that I had left my previous job in Norfolk – and in my mind, the stresses of being employed.

Another vital part of this ceremony of freedom from some of the constrictions of time was to remove my watch, an item I had previously felt quite unable to function without, and toss it with an even bigger flourish into the Grand Union Canal. I watched it slowly sink into the dark waters and I assume it is still there along with the many abandoned traffic cones, tyres, shopping trolleys, guns, washing machines, dead bodies (human and animal) and potentially – as was found in the Stroudwater Canal

Gloucestershire a few years ago – a live crocodile! I also assume the watch has probably ticked its last as it was never particularly reliable, giving up without warning at the first splash of water from an overzealous hand wash, therefore not fit for my new life anyway. Maybe even swallowed by the crocodile. Now I am going into Never-Never land fantasy! My life really did feel like, in the main, an idyllic fantasy in those early days of being together – a fairy tale life that fascinated me.

I read somewhere there is an Amazonian tribe – the Amondawa – whose language has no word for 'time', or indeed of time periods such as 'month' or 'year', and therefore lacks the linguistic structures that relate time and space, as in our idea of, for example, 'working through the night.' I was beginning to enjoy developing this notion for myself, although it caused much consternation to my family, who had no idea where I was or if I was safe at any given time – hence the blogs I wrote in an attempt to keep me connected with them.

Living this novel, almost carefree lifestyle initially felt safe and liberating. I was convinced I had found my true place with the man of my dreams. With hindsight, I'm aware of how anxious I was to maintain this fantasy in a relationship that just under the surface was slowly and methodically chipping away at my real self and indeed my freedom. One of the ways the Labrador would do this was when I tried to persuade him to return from one of his sulks – time spent in self isolation on his own boat. He would lower his voice to a kindly whisper and say how hurt he was and how I just needed to try harder to be kind to him. My friends back in Norfolk, on meeting the Labrador, remarked how he clearly adored me and that was difficult to ignore when I so longed to be adored. My misplaced loyalty towards him prevented me from disillusioning them by telling them of our difficulties – whether this was out of pride or fear of loss took me many years of reflection (and subsequently psychotherapy) to understand.

So, time structuring, along with many other of life's priorities that seemed crucial in my 'old' life, seemed to lose their importance in my new life afloat.

The one thing I was not so delighted to toss into the cut (canal) was my keys. This happened on an occasion when the Labrador was working away in Poland. He often took photography work at exhibitions and trade conferences – sometimes I accompanied him, but often (either due to my work commitments or his reluctance to allow me into this part of his life) he went alone, leaving me to negotiate the challenges of boating life.

We very rarely locked our boats as there was little need to fear burglars on the canal. I think this is partly due to the often mistaken belief that people living on narrowboats have nothing worth stealing. More accurately, I believe boaters tend to look out for each other so if something out of the ordinary was spotted – like someone suspiciously hanging around another's boat – even if you didn't know your 'neighbour', it would be challenged. In my time on the canal, I don't recall hearing about any break-ins. In contrast, I had experienced at least four burglaries when I had lived in a house. Nevertheless, I had not quite felt ready to give up the habit of locking my boat on every occasion I left it. This felt especially reassuring when I was left alone, and funnily enough on this occasion, the only person that broke into my boat was me.

I had locked the rear doors prior to a brief trip into town and was walking along the narrow gunwale (outermost top edge of the boat hull where the deck and hull come together) to reach the rope that had fallen into the water. I recall telling myself to be very careful not to drop my keys into the cut. Moments later, having dropped my keys into the cut and watching them sink slowly into the weeds below, I wondered fleetingly why the cork I had attached to the key ring had not managed to keep them afloat as intended. I guessed it may have been due to the fact that there were at least ten keys on the keyring, including those for my car, my house in Norfolk, both doors of the boat and the British Waterways key (purchased to allow entry to the water points and Elsan facilities where we emptied our cassette toilet). Also, several more I was reluctant to dispose of in case I remembered what they opened in the future.

A dramatic gasp from me (I am particularly proud of my dramatic gasps) as I realised access to my whole life was now at the bottom of the cut. Although the canal is not particularly deep, objects tend to get stuck in weeds below or trapped under the boat or between the side of the boat and the towpath. The upside of my what I now see as a relatively trivial loss was that I whiled away an hour or so pleasantly surrounded by men who seemed to appear from nowhere, keen to relive their boyhood adventures with magnets and fishing lines and to help me out in my dilemma. I never recovered the keys but I gained much more in the process about what was important in life.

I sold or gave away more or less all my material possessions when I took on this new life, including a beautiful Denby dinner service that had taken me years and cost me hundreds of pounds to accumulate, a dishwasher (never really seen the need for these), and many clothes. The only basic boat wardrobe items were a pair of non-slip shoes (the well deck can get treacherously slippery in the rain), gloves for protection when handling lock gates, and two changes of clothes, such as jeans, t-shirts, a warm jumper and a waterproof jacket with hood. All essential as it is so difficult if one set gets wet to dry them speedily without the luxury of a tumble dryer or radiator. (A lesson you may remember I learned earlier on my unplanned diving experience.)

Other things I realised were not necessary to stress over any more:

⚓ No Council Tax – there is an annual boat licence fee that is worked out per foot of the boat but this is tiny in comparison. Seemed very fair to me, having only a small nautical home.

⚓ No TV licence – this is an interesting one which apparently works on an address-based system. When I first moved to Norfolk prior to becoming a boat owner and buying my cottage, I was renting a house. I returned to my original house in my home town of Rugby most weekends to check all was well as it was up for sale. I still had a television there, and another in my rented house. Each Friday evening, I took a wicked pleasure in notifying the TV licensing authority of my change of address and every Monday morning repeated the process in reverse, as I stubbornly rebelled against buying two licences. But no more! Although I had access to TV on my laptop on the boat, to get any sort of reception at all I needed to hang out of the hatch, precariously reach out to the roof and waggle the portable arial with all my might until I could get a half decent picture of anything on the screen and one that didn't look as if it was eternally snowing. However – and this was my ace card – my boat did not have a fixed address...

- ⚓ No weekend trips to the DIY store with the accompanying arguments about which colour paint to buy or curtains and style of furniture to choose.
- ⚓ No ironing clothes. If rumpled badly, they can be naturally pressed with careful folding and positioning under the mattress for a couple of days.
- ⚓ No worrying about endless hair drying, styling, colouring, straightening, curling, etc. (My generator would have expired if I had even attempted to plug in an iron or hair dryer.)
- ⚓ No central heating boiler repairs or costly gas bills.
- ⚓ No visits to expensive garden centres or lawn to mow – the entire countryside was my garden.

All these things I no longer had or indeed needed.

I had always loved being around water, mostly the sea. I had spent many hours sitting in the sand dunes in Winterton wondering at the power of the ocean. It was near to this spot in the sea, at Sea Palling (we had spent family holidays here with our children), where we, several years earlier as a family, had made the emotional journey to scatter the ashes of my late partner. I was absorbed in trying to connect with him in this way, imagining among the grains of sand that had washed up around my feet, parts of him. Only my family will understand the true meaning of 'Let's go and see Pauline.'

Living on a narrowboat presents a different image for me.

A tranquillity – being immersed in the countryside – at one with the seasons and nature.

Gently floating – looking out of a panoramic window on the world, as if a romantic dreamlike figure within a vast landscape painting.

The old images of the busy industrial canals from the past were long gone, replaced with the simplistic beauty and freedom. Spending time savouring mindful breathing in the surprisingly fresh air occupied much of my time now. My deceased partner would have loved the sense of freedom of living this narrowboat life.

So, what else was it that sold this life to me? The contrasts added to the intensity.

A lonely dark and squelchy winter walk home along the towpath on which mud wrestlers would be proud to demonstrate their art – the gradual thawing of cold bones within the warm glow of the quick-to-fire-up pot-bellied stove.

My unwelcome early morning alarm call from the pair of swans persistently and rhythmically tapping the boat with their beaks, hungry for food. My pleasure in feeding them, knowing this would help them and their soon-to-be-hatched young survive a cold night.

I did not know it then, but my coldest night was yet to come.

When people asked me how I spent my time on the boat, my answer was usually, "Just living – pure living as pure as life can be."

REFLECTIONS:

 Weeding is a pointless exercise – the countryside (nature's garden) looks after itself if left alone and it is all the more beautiful for it.

 Life is not just about 'doing' – the 'being' is sometimes more important.

 Memories never go away, they fade – living in the now is more important and all any of us have.

Meet Mellors:
The Original Puss in Boats

'A cat has absolute emotional honesty. Human beings for one reason or another may hide their feelings, but a cat does not.'

Ernest Hemingway

ooking very pleased with himself as only a cat can, Mellors dropped the tiny wide-eyed but lifeless mouse at my feet – the third one that day. I was pleased too. Not at the prospect of dispatching yet another deceased rodent to its watery grave, but because Mellors was happy.

Mellors had been with me since he was a six-week-old kitten. A friend's cat, Flora, had had her second litter in two years and my friend was keen to find homes for them all. I was a reluctant cat owner at first – not because I don't like cats, I love them, but because my partner at the time was a 'dog-man'.

"Just come and see Flora's kittens," my friend said persuasively with that knowing look on her face that only a fellow cat lover can recognise. "You don't have to take one, just come for lunch and a chat."

We ooh'd and aah'd over proud mum Flora, who was a tiny longhaired tabby. It seemed hard to believe she had managed to deliver those six, even tinier miracles. One stood out from the wriggling bundle of fluff in Flora's basket as the only ginger male. The chief suspect in the paternity stakes, having been spotted in the neighbourhood recently, was another ginger cat, almost identical to his son. I looked and I stroked, as much as protective Flora would allow, we ate our lunch, we chatted and I left.

A week later, when my friend visited me for a return lunch, I spotted a tiny pinkish nose peeping out of her pocket.

"Just thought you may want to say hello again," she said. "We have found homes for the other five, but no one seems to want this one. I'll just put him down on this chair while we eat our lunch."

She put the bundle of ginger fur on my partner's favourite chair, where the feline promptly emptied his bladder – and the rest was history.

My partner would never admit he liked Mellors – maybe he had never quite forgiven him for the chair incident. Or maybe it was a secret envy of my relationship with my beloved cat, named by me (if you haven't already guessed) after the handsome gardener in D.H. Lawrence's *Lady Chatterley's Lover*. However, although in public he expressed his dislike of cats, in private it was a different story. I often overheard him in the morning, when he was in the kitchen making a cup of tea before going to work, talking to Mellors about nothing in particular, just as if chatting to a male friend about boys' adventures.

Cats are notorious for imposing themselves on humans they perceive do not like them and Mellors certainly liked him. He was never a lap cat, but loved men's feet and used to sit on my partner's at every opportunity.

When my partner passed away, Mellors noticeably missed him. He would sit for hours in the wooden shed in our garden which my partner had used for his gym equipment. Spookily just staring up at the wall; it was almost as if he could still sense him there.

When I moved to Norfolk, I couldn't initially take Mellors to the house I had rented so he stayed in my house in Rugby, being fed and cared for by my friend, his original 'Mum'. I thought it would be less disruptive for him to stay in familiar surroundings until I was settled. When I could not bear to be without him any longer and towards the end of my tenancy, I collected him to live with me after negotiating with my landlord – who it turned out quite liked cats – our next move being to my own house in Winterton-on-Sea.

Mellors then had to get used to the company of my neighbour's cat. As we were the imposters on their territory, of course there were more than a few scuffles between Mellors and Skimble. Generally, though, Mellors was happy and he had even been spotted lounging on the beach in the sand dunes nearby. I had no intention of moving again and fully imagined that Mellors (at twelve years old) and I would live happily sharing each other's company in sleepy Winterton-on-Sea – Mellors gradually moving towards retirement and me getting accustomed to life without my partner.

Therefore, as you can imagine, I had many concerns for Mellors' happiness when I moved again to live on the boat for my next adventure. He had already had two house moves in two years, so again I was uncertain how he would cope. I thought I would give it a try for a few weeks to see how he settled and then if he didn't, I may have to consider finding him another home on dry land.

On our car journey to the boat, he cried and cried so much I eventually gave in and released him from his cat basket

– a prison cell which held unhappy memories for him of scary vets' visits – hoping he may have a wander around then settle on the seat or the floor. However, Mellors had other ideas and he spent the last hour or so of the journey balanced precariously in front of me on the dashboard, partly obscuring my view through the windscreen. I didn't have the heart to move him and just hoped I didn't get stopped by the police.

On arrival, he spent the first day alternating between sniffing around the boat and curled up on the bed. Mellors soon became brave enough to go out into his huge new garden to explore.

Sitting at my desk on the boat about two weeks later, I was amazed to see a very cautious Mellors pass the window, walking along the gunwales on the canal side. Gunwales vary in width on boats, but on this one they were less than two inches wide!

Mellors did not fall in to the canal on that occasion but did so twice at a later date – he had many an adventure using up several of his nine lives, and I'll tell you more about that later...

REFLECTIONS:

 If you have a need, you have a right to find a way to meet it.

 Not everyone will like you and it doesn't matter – it's all about loving yourself.

 Never stop being curious and exploring.

 Live in the 'now' and never give up the opportunity of a new adventure.

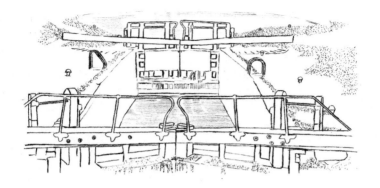

There's
No Place
Like Home

'Toto, I've a feeling we're not in Kansas anymore.'

Dorothy

Screenplay by Noel Langley, Florence Ryerson and Edgar Allan Wolfe from a book by L. Frank Baum (The Wizard of Oz)

I t had been a good day – by which I mean we were getting along OK. I spent it alternating between pottering (a favourite occupation of mine to this day) interspersed with preparation of a training course I was planning to deliver to a nursing home. The course was based on the Dignity in Care Campaign that had been launched around this time by Amanda Waring (the actress daughter of Dorothy Tutin) following her experience of the far from adequate end of life care her mother received. I had also witnessed this lack of dignity and respect shown to vulnerable people in their care by staff in some of the nursing homes and hospitals I had worked in since taking up my self-employed status. This abusive treatment had been heartbreaking to see so I was passionate about implementing this crucial dignity aspect in my training work.

One of the key principles of the campaign stood out for me and is one that I hold dear in my work to this day:

'Enable people to maintain the maximum possible level of independence, choice and control.'

Unfortunately for me at the time, I don't think I realised this principle applied to my relationship. The Labrador had developed subtle ways of taking control of my life in ways that to an outsider may have appeared loving. This odd place I found myself, in between accepting his flattery and adoration and the guilt at 'causing' his anger and distress if I questioned or challenged him was confusing to me.

I now recognise the confusion I experienced as part of his narcissistic manipulation. The seemingly generous help he offered – such as designing my professional website and filling it with his photos of me – would start well with our joint enthusiasm and excitement, then rapidly deteriorate into another fearful shut down. He would spend hours 'perfecting' the photos he had taken of me by smoothing out any minor blemishes on my face. I used to say "Oh that looks better" in order to compliment his painstaking work – surely he must care about me to spend all his time doing this? Actually, deep down this made me feel that my natural appearance wasn't good enough for him so in fact it lowered my self-confidence further. 'Walking on eggshells' is a phrase that I've often heard when in a relationship such as I found myself in with him. I feared disagreeing with him – any minor criticism, particularly about his photography work, would lead to one of his lengthy silences. I often experienced that uneasy sense that I had hurt him.

To relax, one of the ways we might spend some time in the evenings was to play a video game together such as 'Lego Star Wars'. This was a funny game intended for children, I imagine, where the aim was to battle with characters (all made of Lego) to reach the end of the game. When 'shot', the characters would disintegrate and, in true cartoon style, quickly rebuild themselves. I was not particularly proficient at this and I couldn't help thinking it was fortunate they were not real guns – had they been real guns, my inaccurate shooting could have ended very badly. However, it was meant to be fun and a great way of relieving any tensions arising from a particularly difficult day at work. So, when I accidentally 'destroyed' his character, I was quite astonished to realise this was often 'game over' and would lead to another of his silences.

According to the long range weather forecast, there were barely many more sunny good days left in the year. My spirits were much lifted by having Mellors around me. He hadn't taken much to the Labrador and remained mostly on my boat, sleeping during the day on my makeshift desk and occasionally raising his head with annoyance if I disturbed him when I moved my laptop mouse near him.

We had moved to Milton Keynes – a relatively new town founded in 1967 with an aim to relieve the housing pressure in London. The Labrador had appeared to be getting restless in Cowley and started to talk about how beautiful Milton Keynes was. Reluctantly, I had to admit he was right. I'd had my doubts at first, that were based purely on my one brief Christmas shopping expedition to the town, which to me had represented everything I disliked about man-made urban life. With its infamous 'concrete cows' and excessive ever-growing number of roundabouts (as I write this – 130) at the seemingly identical intersections – where I, of course again, got hopelessly lost – it had never been at the top of my list as a place to set up home.

The canalside there, however, surprised me, painting a very different picture: the new and clearly cared for clean gravel towpath, long stretches with no locks to contend with, a strong internet signal, modern Elsan facilities and the beautifully clear water of the canal made it a pleasant contrast to the London end of the Grand Union and somehow I felt less 'grubby' when we were there. And it was peaceful. Away from the madness that is London with its orange halogen glow of the all-night-long street lamps in the distance confusing the wild birds' body clocks into thinking there was eternal daylight and forcing them unnaturally to break into song in the middle of the night. In Milton Keynes, there was even (in one of the many green spaces) an area with its own peace pagoda built next to a Buddhist Temple.

We found our own peaceful spaces as we steadily travelled on our journey from Cowley and through Harefield, Rickmansworth, Kings Langley, Apsley (famous for the paper mills), Hemel Hempstead, Berkhamsted, Marsworth, Linslade and Soulbury. We passed through some of the most beautiful idyllic villages and towns, sampling the local pubs fare as we went. The days were still quite long and we decided to cruise later into the evening, often pushing ourselves beyond tired. Aware we were now way behind schedule, we took shortcuts when operating the locks. Relaxing our grip on the windlass (a metal L-shaped tool with a square socket at one end, used for operating the paddles on lock gates) and allowing it to turn on its own. Working the locks requires considerable effort and taking risks like this can be dangerous – as we heard from a woman we met in Uxbridge who had not been concentrating and the windlass flew off and broke her hip.

One evening, at about 10pm, we happened to moor up for the night by a pub – an instinctive and familiar occurrence for some reason. The seemingly abandoned hostelry looked far from welcoming, and not imagining we would get anything more than a drink and a glare at our muddy boots at that time of night, we went in.

We were surprised to be welcomed warmly by the landlord, and assuming the friendly couple of customers at the bar who were finishing their meal were slow eaters who had ordered much earlier, we just ordered a drink. However, there was still a sizzling sound and the aroma of cooking coming from the kitchen area behind the bar and we were invited by the proud landlord to try some food. In what seemed like only minutes later, the landlord's Thai wife appeared with our drinks and the most authentic curry we have ever tasted.

Not satisfied with that, the landlord then insisted that we sampled a desert – bananas in a coconut milk sauce. All this for the price of a couple of drinks in a town pub and excellent fun and conversation thrown in.

Just prior to moving to Milton Keynes, the Labrador had taken off for a few days to moor a few miles away under a particularly wide bridge of the M25 motorway in order to give his boat a lick of paint.

I spent one night with him there, sleeping on the boat, but quickly returned to my own boat for a good night's sleep – the noise and vibration from the traffic was unbelievable. The only peaceful hours were between 7am-9am and 5pm-7pm, when nothing is moving. The M25 is indeed, as Chris Rea sings, 'The road to hell', and feels no less so when mooring below it than when attempting to drive on it.

We also went up to Brentford – where the Grand Union Canal joins the Thames – and we travelled to Eel Pie Island at Twickenham (again, near the Labrador's home ground before he took to the water). Despite not being able to go further, as our relatively small boats would have struggled on the tidal Thames, these were exciting enough times for me – learning of the history of the island where some of my favourite bands had performed in the sixties, such as The Rolling Stones, The Who and Pink Floyd. Little did I know this would be the last time I would travel to this place (by boat anyway) but I have been lucky enough to see all three bands 'live' at various times in my lifetime.

I'm guessing the Labrador was willing to leave all this behind and move to Milton Keynes, knowing he would return one day, and for me it was one step nearer to my home town of Rugby. So, although I felt less grubby in the pristine Milton Keynes, I longed for the feel of a warm shower, but more importantly, a warm and reassuring hug from my family.

I guess he must have sensed that I was becoming dissatisfied because we hadn't been there long before he decided to fix the shower on his boat. With much deliberation, he managed to order the tiny piece of equipment that had been missing from the boiler for the past – I'm imagining when his boat was built – and was quite insistent that now we could enjoy a refreshing shower, rather than having a 'stand at the sink' wash, there would be no urgent need to visit my family.

In the meantime, my need for 'home' had got stronger. I had become a grandma. At 3am, I got the call from my youngest daughter. Well, it was more of a cross between a grunting sound interspersed with a few choice swear words than a coherent conversation and I deduced from this that 'things' were indeed happening.

My daughter, although living in Leeds, spent much time between there and Barnet (where her partner worked during the week). She had been with us on the boat the previous day as a stop-off point before she headed up to Barnet and we had walked up and down the towpath like a route march – her eating lots of fresh pineapple (apparently, this can induce labour) and me offering lots of other motherly tips and getting secretly more anxious, knowing what she had to come.

So at 3.05am, I mumbled something to the Labrador, who mumbled something back before he went straight back to sleep – clearly not happy with my sudden departure. I grabbed my trusty Sat. Nav., 'Rhoda' – this was certainly not the time to get lost – jumped in my car and broke several speed limits on my way to Barnet Hospital.

Seven pounds and twelve ounces of fantastically, lovely baby granddaughter eventually arrived at 4.54pm following fifteen hours of gruelling labour, which I was privileged to share, although I have to acknowledge my daughter did most of the work. As I took several photos of our new family member, I knew I would want to spend more time with them and felt myself torn apart. My eldest daughter was on holiday in Canada and then returning to her home in Manchester, my stepdaughter was in New York. I pondered how long those trips would take if they were possible on a narrowboat.

No shower, however good – and it was disappointingly no more than a trickle anyway, despite his endless tinkering – could make up for missing my family, from who I felt I was becoming more and more divided.

Then out of the blue, the Labrador got restless again and suggested we go on a cruise up to Leamington Spa...

REFLECTIONS:

 Always ensure you leave enough rope when tying up before entering a lock to allow for the water level to drop. (Not applicable in Milton Keynes.)

 I have the right to be treated with dignity and respect.

 Family love you no matter who you are with or what you are.

 I can allow myself to be relaxed, playful and happy.

The Light At The End Of The Tunnel

- or a bridge too far?

'Man cannot discover new oceans unless he has the courage to lose sight of the shore.'

Andre Gides

eamington Spa was good enough for me as I had done my research and realised we would need to travel on the Grand Union canal to Braunston and then onto the Oxford canal through Clifton-upon-Dunsmore, Hillmorton and Newbold-on-Avon – all in Rugby!

The Labrador was keen to show his prowess at tackling the flight of twenty-one locks that sit together at Hatton in Leamington Spa, known as the 'Stairway to Heaven'. This was one occasion when I wasn't going to argue with him as it certainly felt like I was nearer my heaven, so I humoured him and encouraged him to believe I was keen to go on this latest expedition too.

Maybe he wanted to demonstrate his courage by taking me through the third longest navigable canal tunnel in the UK. Blisworth Tunnel is 3,076 yards long – the ninth longest canal tunnel in the world. At its deepest point, it is around 143 feet below ground level. At only fifteen feet wide, there is no tow path inside and there is just enough room to allow two carefully navigated narrowboats travelling in different directions to pass unscathed. I was, of course, still honing my navigation skills and far from competent. It is probably just as well I wasn't aware of the full history of the tunnel at the time.

Work had begun on the original tunnel in 1793, but there were structural errors made by the contractors, and after three years' work it collapsed due to quicksand, claiming the lives of fourteen men. It was then decided to begin again with a new tunnel. Until the arrival of steam tugs in 1871, travel through the tunnel was only achieved by men – or often women and children – lying on their backs on a plank of wood placed across the bow, pushing the boats with their feet on the walls of the tunnel (a process called 'legging'). Boaters wishing to avoid the extra cost involved in using the tugs could still leg their boats through, but by the 1930s, motorised boats (towing the butty or unpowered boat) were common.

So, pleased my little boat had a reliable engine and I didn't have to 'leg it', truth be told, I was terrified of the journey – much as I longed to reach my destination.

"I always sing," bellowed the jolly voice somewhere from the boat moored on the other side of the canal at the entrance to the tunnel.

Looking across from my boat, I saw the owner of the voice was a sturdy looking woman dressed in khaki shorts and hiking boots, who reminded me of my old Guide Mistress, not just in stature or because of the dark shadow across her upper lip, but the way her booming voice immediately made me feel the need to stand to attention and salute. I did not have happy memories of the Guides. I had long since decided the camping lifestyles of Guides was not for me. Sharing a tent with six other smelly girls, being stung by a wasp who had decided to take up residence on my jam sandwich, and all set in a field full of cows with a hole in the ground for a toilet left me traumatised and averse to camping to this day. Even to the point of turning down a lifetime wish for a trip to the Glastonbury Festival because I couldn't book into a hotel and have room service.

As I daydreamed about these memories, they temporarily took my mind off the task in hand and brought into my awareness the fact that I was now actually living this natural life outdoors and enjoying it – mostly. However, her freely and loudly offered advice jolted me to the reality of what I was about to do and sounded a good idea for two reasons.

Firstly, because I think making any noise is good when you are scared – the louder the better. Secondly, my singing voice has been likened to that of a very sick cat and I was certain it would warn oncoming boaters well in advance of my approaching, even over the sounds of our engines.

The Labrador had given me another piece of useful advice regarding travelling in a tunnel. I pulled up the hood of my waterproof coat to protect myself from the constant drip of icy cold water from the roof of the tunnel, which apparently without warning intermittently turns into a deluge to shock the back of your neck.

Having flicked the switch to turn on the navigation lights, in a barely audible, wobbly voice, I said to Mellors, "Right mate, we're going in." Of course, he was out of earshot anyway, having adopted his usual comfortable place, curled up on my bed.

Becoming disorientated in that first few minutes on entering the black abyss, all my childhood fears came back to me – and a few adult ones too. However, forward was the only way to go. I could not go back and I needed to get to Rugby. There are no diversions on the canal, no alternative routes. Oh, how I longed for an alternative at that point – even Rhoda the Sat. Nav. couldn't have helped me – it was onward or nothing.

On this breathtakingly sunny day, the thought of leaving the light in exchange for the terrifyingly dark unknown ahead was, I imagined, a little like being born, only in reverse. Well, actually not quite, as the womb is supposedly a slightly more inviting and warm place. The pitch-black tunnel loomed ahead of me, rather tauntingly – far from inviting.

I don't normally talk to anyone when I am scared but I trusted that Mellors never questioned my fears any more than I did his (see frog episode in later chapter). So even though he couldn't hear me as he was fast asleep on my bed, having a one-way conversation with him about nothing in particular calmed my nerves further. This went something like:

"Are you looking forward to going home, mate? I am. I can't wait to see the family again. Is it true cats can see better in the dark? Well you could get off the bed and help me out here."

I have since established that my use of the term 'mate' is one of my indicators that I am scared as it is not a term of address I usually employ. Once, when driving back from a nightclub in Norwich late at night (unhappily widowed and pre Labrador days), I had just left a multi storey car park and, as I checked my rear view mirror, was horrified to see I was being pursued by a flashing blue light, complete with police car underneath.

Now unusually, I had not taken any alcohol that day, or for that matter, any other substances that may have attracted the interest of the law, so was not concerned about being breathalysed. I was not even sure if they were trying to attract my attention or if they were chasing a real criminal; either way, I thought I had better pull over.

As the extremely young (about fifteen in my estimation) and I have to admit, rather attractive looking policeman approached my car, I wound down my window with a shaky hand and launched into what can only be described as a tirade of gibberish.

"How are you, mate?" I began.

Never having met me before, he seemed a little surprised at my familiarity, which I can only guess was my desperate attempt to establish some sort of friendship with him. Maybe not a bad idea, given his good looks, although it didn't quite seem to be having the impact in the way I might have hoped.

He was not even slightly deterred by my fruitless advances and persevered with his policeman's script, in true bureaucratic style.

"And where have we been this evening, madam?"

I often wonder how the use of the first person plural by officials of any sort adds to the gravity of the situation, but it does seem to.

"Oh, just out with friends, mate," I rambled on, racking my brains to remember what possible crime I might have committed on the streets of Norwich during this seemingly uneventful evening out.

He then decided, having at last been able to get a word in, to enlighten me as to my crime. (Pardon the pun – see next line).

"Are you aware, madam, that you have no lights showing on your vehicle?"

"Oh, thank you, thank you so much for telling me. They are working, mate, I just forgot to switch them on,"

I gushed, almost taking off a passing cyclist's ear in my hurry to get out of the car (after switching on the offending headlamps) to check they were now visible.

My biggest fear about navigating through the tunnel was that I would meet another boat coming the other way and we would have a head-on collision. In a car, of course, the outcome of this event at even 30mph could be a lot worse than two boats travelling at less than a quarter of that speed. However, it is still distressing to think about the possibility of crashing and damaging your or someone else's home. I hoped that another more experienced boater would see my lights in good time and be a little better, in the very small space available, at navigating and avoiding this catastrophe.

If you stay very much to the right, you cannot really go far wrong, apart from the occasional scraping of the side of the boat on the slimy rough walls of the tunnel. This posed more of a risk for me, having lost a couple of side fenders – beautiful buffers traditionally crafted from rope – in a previous incident which I won't go into now. Only to assure you, in case you were wondering, that of course it wasn't my fault.

As I settled a little into this strange new and unfamiliar world, I could not begin to imagine how tough it must have been to navigate the working boats carrying coal, etc., through the tunnels. Having no towpaths in the tunnels, and prior to motorisation, getting the canal boat through would have involved 'legging', as mentioned earlier. The horse that would normally pull the boat would be led on the road over the tunnel to meet the boat when it emerged on the other side.

This thought then brought the additional worry as to

what would I do if Argy's engine failed midway. I thought this an ideal time to take heed of the wise words of 'sturdy woman' and I broke into song. A particularly weak version of 'Jerusalem' was followed by an almost as shaky 'I Vow to Thee My Country', although by the time I got to 'Land of Hope and Glory' I had gathered both momentum and courage and was travelling at an incredible four knots – pushing Argy's capacity beyond his limits in my eagerness to get out of this seemingly never-ending hell.

I successfully negotiated, without more than a scratch (I am convinced their fault not mine), the passing of two holiday boats, both containing revellers dressed as pirates and drinking cans of beer. Always a slightly unwelcome sight on the canal, but in the darkness, even more unnerving.

Fast running low on songs I knew all the words to and my one-sided conversation with Mellors becoming dull in this darker-than-a-coal-mine place, finally I became aware that the tiny pinhead-sized dot of hopeful light in the distance that I was fixated on was gradually becoming bigger. Eventually emerging into the dazzling sunlight of a perfect summer day after this half an hour cruise, I felt a little like a rabbit caught in headlights, half expecting someone to capture my startled expression on camera (as they do at theme parks when you are terrifyingly hurtling downhill on some blood curdling ride like the water chute or Big Dipper).

Admittedly feeling rather smug at achieving another boating challenge, I shakily reapplied my (by this stage) rather smudged lipstick (a narrowboating essential kept in my pocket at all times) and continued with renewed hope on my journey to Rugby.

REFLECTIONS:

 There is always a light at the end of the tunnel and we will eventually find it.

 Guides of all varieties are often around where you least expect to find them and have some very sound ideas and techniques for survival.

 Worrying doesn't solve anything.

 I am braver and more capable than I think I am.

 I also have the right to feel scared and to say, "I'm afraid."

Froggies, Doggies And Moggies:

My family and other animals

'When you see a snake,
never mind where he
came from.'

William Gurney Benham

T hings seemed so much brighter now that much of my family was almost within walking distance. Even the Labrador seemed to take to Rugby and our temporary mooring at Clifton-upon-Dunsmore and thoughts of moving on to Leamington Spa were certainly far from my mind – and it seemed his too.

We went to my step-grandson's belated birthday barbeque, and even though it didn't seem like I had been away for long, it seemed time was moving on without me – my two step-granddaughters, having just started 'big school'.

I caught up with three old friends from my counselling training days. I didn't realise how much I had missed them. It was very tempting to book a bath or shower at their houses, but I was too proud to ask, not wanting them to think I was anything but happy with my new lifestyle. One, whilst giving her usual greeting hug, sprang away from me, shouting 'how long?' when I told her we had not showered since we moved onto the boats. I hoped her reaction wasn't because my smell confirmed the fact.

Mellors also seemed very comfortable to spend the time in his original home territory. He was now very confident wherever we were. It was a regular occurrence to find many daily 'presents' of tiny mice from his hunting expeditions in his own personal jungle all along whichever towpath we were moored at the time.

As far as I remember, Mellors had never caught anything very much bigger than a mouse; the only exception to this being when he was about twelve weeks old when he captured the biggest blackbird I have ever seen. In our home in Winterton, he was particularly partial to the odd less challenging prey such as a butterfly or flying leaf. So, when I was suddenly awoken by a squeaking noise around 3am one morning, I assumed it was just another unfortunate tiny rodent Mellors had taken a fancy to. The at first insignificant squeak rapidly developed into a loud, shrill ear-piercing scream unlike any sound I had ever heard before. In my half-awake/half-asleep state, for a split second I thought there was a howling baby on the boat. I hid under the duvet screaming, "Get it out, get it out," pushing the Labrador out of bed to send him courageously searching the boat with a stick (no idea what he thought he was going to do with this) in one hand and a torch in the other. There was a lot of scuffling and a fair bit of swearing. I peeped out just in time to see, in the light of the torch, the 'mouse' leaping through the air. It took me another few seconds to realise that mice don't really have the acrobatic prowess to jump that high and that it was, in fact, a frog. The sheer volume of its blood-curdling shrieks succeeded in frightening Mellors, who was by this time long gone and I imagine making him wish he had never thought of the idea of attempting to catch a more troublesome and vocal prey.

When we spoke to our towpath neighbours the next day, they very diplomatically said they had not heard the frog, but had heard my loud, desperate screams to the Labrador. I blushed every time I saw them after this and, although they were very friendly, I was quite relieved when they moved on further up the cut.

Another episode that tested my courage was when I had my first ever close up sighting of what I thought was a grass snake. Apparently, in the sand dunes in Winterton, there were adders, and although they are the UK's only venomous snake, their bite is not dangerous. However, the bite area can become quite painful and inflamed. I was always anxious walking on the dunes as I have an acute fear of snakes and it never entered my head that I would encounter one near the canal. I don't have any memory of where this fear came from, although the story my mum delighted in telling everyone was of the time when I had (at about age three) walked into the house from our garden to show her the pretty patterned lifeless 'necklace' I had found and was wearing proudly around my neck. I obviously wasn't afraid then and I'm imagining it was her terrified look, probably accompanying much hysterical screaming and shouting, that implanted the fear in my unconscious memory forever.

This specimen that now slithered swiftly across my path on an early morning walk was at least two feet long and quickly disappeared into the wooded area at the side of the towpath. The Labrador's response, when I tearfully relayed the story of the by then 'forty-foot snake' to him, was dismissive: "It was probably a slow worm. I expect he was more afraid of you than you were of him." A thought occurred to me (although I was getting quite adept at storing these firmly in the back of my mind): If this man can dismiss my fears so easily, does he really care about me?

Aside from these relatively mild clashes with wildlife, and with the more frequent visits to and from my family and friends, I found being this close to nature fascinating and it made life with the Labrador much more bearable.

Another step-grandson joined us and enjoyed some early morning fishing from the boat, catching two fish with a makeshift rod of wood and line. It is so funny to watch pieces of bread moving around as if by remote control, the fish hidden under the water pushing them.

There is so much that goes unnoticed when visiting the canalside, that can be pondered at a much slower pace from the peace of a narrowboat. I'll always remember the russet beauty of the Muntjac deer that fearlessly swam from one side of the canal to disappear into the bushes on the other side. No time to get out my camera to capture this rare event.

I had never really understood the point of fishing before. My theory was, to amuse myself, that there was only a couple of fish in the entire canal and they were repeatedly caught and thrown back. However, having watched the many fisherman on the towpath who sit peacefully and patiently for days on end, I get it. It's the 'not doing' that's allows the space for reflective thinking. Keeping busy has little purpose other than to avoid our deep thoughts and stresses – peaceful reflections are much more relaxing and indeed effective when mulling over a problem.

Nature also has its cruel side. I was always throwing crumbs of bread to distract the male ducks who often aggressively tried to mate with the females to the point of sometimes drowning them. Swans can also be quite vicious, especially when protecting their young, and baby swans and ducks are at risk from the herons who noiselessly wait like evil-looking statues to capture their spoils.

While we were minding our own business, other passers-by were not always so polite. Known as 'gongoozlers', these are people who watched, took an interest in canals and canal life, but didn't participate in the physical activities such as offering to help us open the heavy lock gates. This can be quite irritating at the end of a very long day's cruising, when the gates feel even heavier and you hear the words "I bet you're tired doing that all day?" Or worse – "It must be lovely not to have to go to real work."

Aside from my previously mentioned passing boater's comments about Argy's name and the kind but misguided enquiries about the temperature and dryness of a boat in winter, I came across a few other judgemental remarks in my time on the water.

"Can you read and write?" Not really sure about the reasoning behind this one. Maybe they thought that there's no need for literary skills for such a simple lifestyle.

"Do you have a job or are you claiming benefits?" This one was particularly stinging, given my strong work ethic.

But it was not just words that were irritating. I often emerged from my bed on Sunday morning to see half a dozen or so East-Asian tourists taking photographs of Argy. There would be great excitement when they saw me, and they would call more of their friends down, wanting me to pose for photos with them on my boat. I felt like a celebrity, even thought about getting a piece of red carpet for the well deck. Still, at least they saw a more authentic picture of our lives as boat dwellers.

Mellors, however, was unlike me, not concerned about politeness when responding to these intrusions on our privacy, and was becoming very protective of me – and not just against potential harm from a Labrador.

For some unknown reason, people walking their dogs along the towpath (and there are a lot of them) did not seem to understand that the boats moored there are, in the main, people's homes. I often wondered how they might feel if I had entered their gardens and stared through the windows of their houses. I was seriously thinking of getting a sign for my boat saying 'BEWARE – DOGS ENTER AT YOUR OWN RISK'. Of course, dogs can't read, but I lived in hope that at least some of their owners could.

Unfortunately for one dog with one not-so-thoughtful owner, what happened one day made me think such a notice might be unnecessary after all. Always a grumpy cat, on this particular day, Mellors must have been feeling especially cantankerous – or maybe his hormones were giving him some trouble. (Do cats have hormones?) Whatever the reason, he seemed to have made it his life's work to protect me and my boat from all creatures great and small. A tiny, very boisterous and friendly puppy (whose owner had obviously cut loose from her lead) decided out of puppy curiosity to take a look in my well deck. Mellors, as usual curled and snoring on his cushion, ears back, almost instinctively preparing for battle in his sleep, flexing his claws and licking his lips. I leapt from my chair as I recognised the low growl that Mellors was emitting. Now in his teenage years, I was confident from previous experience in our sometimes troubled parent/ child relationship that this was definitely not an expression of welcome in cat language. Before I could say "Get down, Shep", there was a loud yelping noise – from the puppy,

I presumed – and a very concerned dog owner who had suddenly appeared from nowhere (a little late if you ask me) was demanding an explanation as to why I could not keep my cat under control! I attempted a frown at Mellors but it was a pathetic effort and I think it came out as more of a smile. The owner stormed off, dog in tow and now safely on a lead that she had miraculously and belatedly produced from a pocket. As the puppy shook his head in the distance, I noted a considerable splattering of his blood flying through the air. Result!

Mellors gave a satisfied purr, went back to sleep and calm was restored… until the next time he was required to take the dog watch.

Little did I realise I was heading for even more argy bargy.

REFLECTIONS:

 Animal disputes have a way of sorting themselves out – not so quickly human ones.

 There are two reasons why we forget; either the event is insignificant or it is so awful we bury it deep in our unconscious.

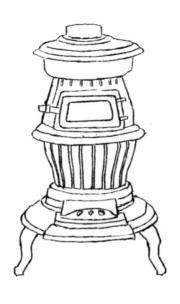

'You're Gonna
Be Happy,' said Life,
'But first I'll make you strong'

Paul Coelho

'I tried to drown my sorrows but the bastards learned how to swim.'

Frida Kahlo

don't recall the actual moment it started to go very wrong but I do recall the sense he was gradually discarding me.

I was on a visit to a friend and when I returned to where our boats were moored, his had gone. I thought at first he may have gone to fill up with water so I called his mobile.

I called again – I lost count of the number of times – and eventually he responded, days later, saying he thought I'd be OK now I was back home and he didn't feel comfortable staying in one place. That was it.

I had no ideas where he was and I spent many hours walking along the towpath to see if I could spot him, without success. The weather was changing. I was getting anxious as to how I was going to manage on my own. I couldn't return to my home in Norfolk as my tenant was still refusing to budge or pay any rent and I had to accept reluctantly he had no intention of doing either. According to my solicitor, it would take at least nine months to get him out and that was if all went well with the legal proceedings.

As they were nearly all nearby, I could have stayed with family, but it didn't seem feasible for more than a few days and my pride wouldn't let me anyway.

I had never been alone on my boat for more than a couple of days and had no idea what to do if things went wrong. And I missed him. This time alone afforded me time to think but the thoughts just went round and round in my head. His complete lack of communication led me to feel yet again that I had done something wrong and now, even more distressingly, with no knowledge of his whereabouts, I had no way of attempting to put it right. Previous to this sudden departure, he had never stopped talking about me to others in a way that sort of felt good. I now felt confused and shocked. What could I possibly have done to have made him leave me?

After about a week, I had to acknowledge he was not coming back. I rallied all my strength and moved my boat from Clifton to Hillmorton Locks, where I wouldn't have to move as far to get water or empty the toilet. I decided to try to adapt to life on my own and to make a decision about the future after I had experienced the challenge of a winter alone on my boat. It would be a test of my resilience and what an achievement if I could do it alone.

There was a small café at the locks and I decided to try to make friends with the owners (a couple), and without appearing too needy – although I was beginning to feel it – see what support I might get. The couple prided themselves on their 'bistro', as they called it, and in their home cooked food from a limited menu of full English breakfast, chips, burgers, lasagne, curry and a very tasty Sunday lunch. The opening hours were also somewhat limited and seemed to vary according to the mood of the chef rather than to fit the sign on the door. It was, however, somewhere to spend my evenings and to get a meal – although it was pot luck to guess what time they stopped serving.

My own efforts at cooking on my boat and my menu was even more limited than theirs. I would usually throw together an omelette or a bacon sandwich. It just didn't seem worth bothering just for myself. So, it was more for company than to eat that I would end up most evenings sitting at the bar with a glass of Shiraz and chatting to the couple of locals – non boat-dwellers – who also dropped in. However, I felt very much the 'outsider' with my lack of knowledge about boating, and being a 'lone' woman. Feeling vulnerable and less than comfortable to share my story – and there was little interest in it from them in any case – I probably drank more wine than was good for me and this lowered my mood even more.

To add to my misery, it was one of these evenings that led to me tearing a ligament in my foot. John from the bistro often allowed me to take a glass of wine back to my boat when, later in the evening, I couldn't even bear the company of the few people at the bistro any more. As I stepped into the well deck of my boat, my foot slipped and twisted badly under me. Within minutes, the blue and purple swelling on the top of my foot had grown to cricket ball proportions. Unspilled glass of a particularly rich red wine still in my hand, I felt nauseous from the pain, both physical and emotional. I sat on the floor of the well deck and sobbed. This was my lowest point. The only way was up!

Probably a bad decision, but the following morning I felt there was no option but to drive myself to the local A and E department. I must have looked a sorry sight as my foot was strapped up and I was given a Zimmer frame to walk with. This was no use whatsoever on my boat as it barely fitted through the door.

So, to add to my misery, I now felt like an elderly disabled woman, hobbling around as best I could, longing for the romance and companionship I had enjoyed when I initially set off on my adventure with the Labrador. Even the warm balmy sunny days were getting fewer and shorter and there was a definite chill in the air and in my heart.

I'm guessing the seasonal change was one of the reasons why there was a noticeable absence of visitors beating their way along the towpath to my boat. Warm sunshine glistening on the water and baby ducks are very enticing – cold, dark evenings and damp, gloomy narrowboats not so.

My eldest daughter called in on her way from her home in Manchester to a work meeting in London. It was great to see her, if only to give her the opportunity to vent her worries about my lifestyle. She also tried to press me, should I move my boat again, into giving her some sort of more precise entry for her address book, which proved a little more difficult. 'The third bridge after the Black Swan pub a few feet down from the water point, opposite the field with the sheep in' cut no ice with her and she left mumbling something about wondering why I could not live in a house like a normal mother and I'd better let her know in plenty of time if I would like a hair dryer for Christmas. I would have loved the luxury of a hair dryer, but of course this was completely out of the question, as my boat batteries would expire completely with more than a few minutes' usage.

I think it reassured her a little when her mobile phone rang during her visit and she left with the (mistaken) belief that mine also would have a strong enough signal should

I need to call her in an emergency. I thought it best not to disillusion her by telling her that it might be necessary to climb onto Argy's roof and wave my arms around for this miracle of the modern age to actually happen for me.

Most nights I was restless and was often awake at dawn looking out over the water at the eerie mist that hung just above the water's surface, signifying the difference in temperature between the air above and water below. This showed the nights were indeed getting colder and it would take a little more forward planning and extra work to keep warm, rather than simply flicking a central heating switch as you would in a house.

However, I thought I was well prepared when I returned from a particularly challenging training job in London – the bistro owners had kindly offered to feed Mellors while I was away and he was, as always, ambivalent on my return. I was getting used to coping with the long, dark winter evenings and was looking forward to a glass of Shiraz and a cosy night in with John Humphrys (Radio 4). I was aware that I was drinking more than was good for me, and although my humour still kept me afloat, there was a ruefulness to it at that time. I had a very large log that I had proudly foraged from a nearby hedgerow, a family size box of matches and a pack of 'Tesco's Finest' firelighters. I knew the firelighters were cheating, again remembering my guiding days, but to be fair, I did leave the Guides early, immediately following the aforementioned camping experience and before I had the chance to take my fire lighting badge. So, I thought, given the circumstances, I deserved a few luxuries.

I didn't have very much water in Argy's tank, not having the time to fill up before I went away, or much gas in the cylinder that was used to light my tiny gas hob and oven. My neighbours, it appeared, had moved on to the next village while I was away in London. So, I was indeed truly alone as I stepped onto my boat that evening on the coldest night of the year so far. I was still feeling more than a little sorry for myself.

Not to be discouraged, I set to, to fire up the little pot-bellied stove. I put in the firelighter covered with some carefully folded newspaper – homemade log style as I had learned from the Labrador – and a few twigs from the towpath for kindling. Then, for my *pièce de résistance*, the super log! I pushed and shoved, twisted and turned but the damn thing was too big to fit through the tiny opening of the stove. Do you know how long it takes to saw through a large log with a rather rusty handsaw? I do, but I was on a mission and somehow, I managed it.

A couple of hours later – by the time I had used all my kindling and got down to my last firelighter and penultimate match – I had begun to realise that there might be another problem. The fire seemed to spark up well then fizzle out just as quickly. It just wasn't drawing. By now it was around 11pm and I was tired and thirsty. The temperature was dropping by the minute, it seemed to alarmingly low levels. I put the kettle onto the two-ringed gas hob, looking forward to a cup of tea to warm me up. The water heated to about lukewarm before the gas flame that was gradually getting weaker and weaker finally spluttered and died despite my willing it to keep going with a few choice words uttered through chattering teeth.

Mindful that now the only thing I could do to avoid the inevitable onset of hypothermia was go to bed, comforted by the soothing voice of the shipping forecast broadcaster, the relaxing music of 'Sailing By' and a cup of cold red wine, I piled on all the clothes I could find, including scarf, hat and gloves, and got into my tiny bed just as the shipping forecaster's voice crackled and died, along with my radio's battery – and I have to admit, at that point, any of my remaining spirit for narrowboating.

The next morning, however, I gained new determination. When I finally thawed out enough to open the hatches, I was greeted by the most beautiful, magical, glittery frosty morning. I was back to my old self. My enthusiasm for this strange, self-imposed, secluded lifestyle returned. I could think straight once I had stretched out and could feel my legs and I went for the best tasting cup of tea I can ever remember at a local supermarket while I pondered my plight. I also bought one of those logs made of packed sawdust, guaranteed to burn for four hours.

When I got back to Argy, I decided to tackle the problem of the fire. I took my trusty barge pole from the roof – an item no longer needed to move the boat along, but one that comes in very handy to aid manoeuvres when stuck in the mud. I pushed it down Argy's chimney as hard as I could, and sure enough, when I looked in the stove, there was a big wad of soggy leaves. "Yes!" I whooped and punched the air, forgetting that the roof was only six inches above my head. Even my bruised hand could not deter me from my joy and my own smartness at resolving the problem.

I set to and lit 'the log' – which, contrary to the previous night's experience, caught immediately, producing a glowing orange flame. I snuggled down onto the bed and must have fallen asleep, because the next thing I remember was a roaring noise in my ears. When I came to, I was dripping with sweat. Flames were coming out of the top of the stove and Argy resembled the 'Towering Inferno'. The thought fleetingly crossed my mind of where I was going to get some water before I came to my senses and managed to grab a bucket and fill it with water from the cut, throwing enough at the stove to cause the flames to sizzle and die.

Following this incident, I did wisely buy a fire extinguisher, just to be on the safe side. Why on earth didn't they put clearer safety instructions on those logs? 'Not to be used on narrowboats!' I have a feeling there might have been something on the crumpled packaging that I found under the bed a few days later. Nevertheless, I was so relieved that Mellors and I had survived another day – although I sensed there may be 'colder' days to come.

REFLECTIONS:

 Always read the instructions – alternatively, keep a fire extinguisher handy.

 Aloneness is not the same as loneliness.

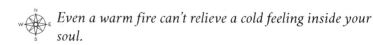 *Even a warm fire can't relieve a cold feeling inside your soul.*

How Was
Your Day?

'When it comes to housework, the one thing no book of household management can ever tell you is how to begin. Or maybe I mean why.'

Katharine Whitehorn

A lthough I was often 'alone' with the Labrador when he 'ghosted me', my actual physical aloneness was different. I felt completely lost. There was more bad news to come when I visited the café one morning and saw the notice on the door which read:

'We will be taken our annual break and the
bistro will be closed for two months from tomorrow.
We reopen on February 1st and wish all our
customers a Merry Christmas.'

I felt defeated, alone and lost.

We had spent the previous Christmas on the Labrador's boat, enjoying the (I have to say) very tasty half goose he had prepared. It was half because we shared the original full sized version with our neighbours, neither of us having a big enough oven on our boats to be able to accommodate a whole bird. The Labrador originally had asked me if I would like to try swan! He had some strange ideas. I was unsure if this was either advisable, given my delicate stomach, or for that matter, legal. So, I declined, once again 'hurting his feelings' by refusing his idea. I was quite relieved, therefore, when our neighbours offered the plump goose – letting me off the hook from more days of silence just before Christmas.

Devoid of human company, I reminisced in my usual one-sided conversation with Mellors (who, as always, was totally uninterested and snoring on my bed) about the times when my partner was alive and Christmases were big family affairs. Clutching the mug I had bought for my partner as a joke as it had a picture of a ginger cat on, I wondered if this time of year for me would ever be as happy again.

We had lived in a large Victorian house and enjoyed not only inviting the extended family to our get-togethers, but often a few waifs and strays who had nowhere to go. A friend who had been 'dumped' by his girlfriend on Christmas Eve or a neighbour who had recently lost his wife. There was always more than enough food and certainly more than enough drink flowing, and creatively thinking of a last-minute present to give our unexpected visitors was always fun.

My thoughts became darker – I now felt like a waif and stray as I recalled a chilling stark memory from our time in Cowley. We didn't know him well, the man who died, although we had seen him around on the towpath at Cowley and knew he lived on a rather run-down and unloved looking boat just up from where ours were moored. The first we knew about his death was when a policeman arrived at his boat early one morning, followed by two paramedics struggling and stumbling along the towpath with a covered trolley. Out of respect, we didn't watch the rest. I was beginning to understand the harsh reality of living alone and could only imagine the dreadful experience of what it would be like to die alone.

I found it quite fascinating to make up my own narratives about why some of the boat dwelling people we encountered had chosen to take to this lifestyle. In the main, the people we met lived alone on their boats. Often divorced or widowed, sometimes having come through life-changing experiences or illnesses, and there were couples too, retired and finding (as I thought I had) a way out of the 'rat race'.

Pouring another glass of Shiraz – probably not helpful to raise my mournful mood – I hopefully prodded the dying embers of the fire in the stove in an attempt to squeeze a little more heat from them. Another disturbing image came slowly came back to me from when I was a district nurse and I was asked to sit through the night with a woman in her sixties who was terminally ill. However, as my children were small at the time and with no one available to care for them and no one else available to sit with her, I agreed to visit as early as I could the next morning. When I arrived, she had clearly died some hours before and had been found by a neighbour who had called the undertaker. They stood coldly around her bed, clearly irritated that they couldn't continue with their job until I could locate a doctor to certify her death.

These memories, and the stark thought of dying alone, I'm sure contributed to my greater need to establish much more contact with my nearby family. I had asked one of my stepsons to call to repair one of my boat's hatches where the hinge had become loose. I'm imagining this may have seemed a small unimportant job to him but I was afraid it would break off altogether and be lost in the cut before he could get some time off from his work to fix it. So, I'd kept the hatch closed for a few weeks, making my boat feel even more gloomy and dark.

Sadly, I'd sensed that for my family nearby, the novelty of visiting my boat had probably worn off and those who lived further afield were preoccupied with their own busy lives – although I knew they were worried about me.

The temptation to isolate myself balanced with the need for company and connection – always a difficult dilemma for me which subsequently took many years of personal therapy to understand.

Thankfully, it turned out most of my Christmas was not spent alone that year, having taken up invitations from my daughters and step family. I did have Mellors to think about, though. With no one around to feed him on days when I was working away and now for some of the Christmas break, I had to find a cattery to take him. This was not without challenges – for him and for me. However, that is a story for later.

My way of affording myself less time to think and avoid experiencing my painful feelings was to keep myself occupied with what my friend calls 'Dorising'. I am presuming that this term has a capital 'D' and originated from a very clean, house-proud woman called Doris – unless anyone knows differently? Dorising narrowboat style goes something like this... About once a week, I needed to take Argy to the water point to fill up his tank. It was important that these manoeuvres were not attempted on a windy day as Argy, wilful as he was, could not cope with even the slightest puff of wind without completely losing his sense of direction. I found this out to my cost one day as I hurtled sideways down the cut for about 500 yards before managing to regain some measure of control of him. Fresh water had to be fetched weekly as Argy's tank was quite small and when getting near empty, he became lighter on one side (Portside, I think it is called?) and took on a very unnerving dip to the left. This made sleeping in my tiny bed quite uncomfortable and disorientating and I had to bolster several cushions up against the wall to counteract the sensation that I was sleeping on the side of a mountain.

This essential water collection process usually began with my trying to get Mellors on board. It seemed the moment the thought came into my mind about moving the boat, his mind-reading powers kicked in and he decided to go for a walk along the towpath. I often spent a good half hour trying to coax him back with treats and sweet talk, none of which I meant and none of which he was fooled by. Eventually, when and only when he deemed it acceptable and I was suitably irritated, he would jump back onto the boat and settle himself onto my bed for the journey. I needn't have worried, as once I got so impatient with him I left him sitting on the towpath. When I returned, over an hour later, he was still sitting in the same spot. I never had the heart to do that again.

On arriving at the water point, assuming there was a space to tie up, I attached the hose to the tap on the towpath and put the other end into the opening of the tank on the front of Argy. This involved climbing onto the sharp end and balancing precariously as I unscrewed the cover to the tank, being careful not to drop the cap into the cut, thus avoiding another 'key' incident. I was never the best at 'parking' my boat, similarly my car, given my more or less complete lack of spatial awareness. The first time I proudly drove my car alone immediately after passing my driving test, eager to show off around town, only resulted in me driving around for quite a while before returning home because I couldn't find a space big enough to manoeuvre into. In a narrowboat, my skills had not improved much. My efforts were often accompanied by shouts of 'Whoa' from other boaters who were concerned about scratches to their paintwork.

While filling up, I took the opportunity to wash my hair at the large ceramic sink, an operation which takes a fair amount of water and would (had I waited until I got back to my mooring) have resulted in an almost empty tank again. To make this operation slightly more aesthetically pleasant, I used one of those cream painted tin jugs adorned with red and yellow roses that have come to be recognised as traditional narrowboat art. I would throw the rubbish I had brought with me into the skip provided next to the water point and then take a deep breath before facing the next not so delightful job of emptying the cassette toilet.

Entering the little hut – the floor of which was swimming in what I sincerely hoped was just water – I had mastered the art of holding my breath for the entire procedure. The secret of rinsing out the toilet after emptying was to try to gauge the water pressure from the tap, which varied enormously from minute to minute. Too little and the job took ages and was not thorough enough. Too much and believe me when I say that's probably all the detail you need to hear of this part of my story.

By this stage, the water tank would be full and I'd turn Argy around to return to my usual parking spot. This was the easy part as he was small enough to be turned using just the ropes attached to the front and rear. A bit of swift lassoing went on and providing I had remembered to remove the chimney pot beforehand – which could have easily been dislodged with my poor roping skills and lost to the cut – this was usually a fairly trouble-free procedure. Apart from the time when I delayed replacing a rather worn rope and he broke free and set off on his own down the centre of the cut only to be rescued and towed back to me by a wonderful boater I can't remember the name of but to whom I am extremely grateful to this day.

Once securely tied up – assuming the mooring pins were still where I left them – I needed to charge the batteries further before I could start the remainder of the day's work on my laptop. A short trip like that was not enough for a day's internet browsing. Before I could start to run the small back-up generator, I had to change the oil. I would never have known this, had the man who sold it to me not told me as he sucked in his cheeks and shook his head. (I thought only car mechanics did that). "You need to change it after every fifty hours' use or you'll bugger it up, and we won't be responsible."

One day, I emptied the old oil into a very small container through an even smaller funnel and refilled with fresh. But when I went to put the petrol in the generator, the can was completely empty. I had forgotten to pick some up from the garage when I filled up my car the day before. So, then I was off on a fifteen-minute walk to the car, petrol can in hand. I thought I might as well take the washing to the launderette while I was out.

Three hours later, back on Argy, I had finally finished the chores I needed to complete just to start the day. I switched on my laptop. It was now about 5pm and I was not really feeling much like work, so I thought a cuppa might be nice. Filling the kettle, I tried to turn on the gas and ... nothing! I knew I should have got a replacement when the last one ran out and I had completely forgotten about it, leaving me with two empty gas bottles.

I had to climb on to the front of the boat in the dark and fiddle with a spanner to disconnect the gas bottle, lugging one of the empty ones out on to the towpath (they are not light, even when empty), to take on a trolley to the chandlery for a replacement. The chandlery, by the way – for those of you who have not completely lost interest by now – was near where I had got the water from that morning.

I eventually returned to Argy around 6pm. Making the tea, I was thinking it was far too late to start work now, so I took that good book I had been meaning to read for ages, lay on my now perfectly level bed, and wondered how I ever found the time to work.

Addendum. I later found a wonderful and enterprising woman called Mary, who in exchange for a meagre amount, would take away my washing and return it a couple of days later, beautifully clean, dry, pressed and folded. Luxury!

Reflections:

 Why was I so resistant to asking for help? I realise now it is not a sign of weakness but of strength.

 Spontaneity is great fun but sometimes it's helpful to have some structure too, and a well thought-out plan.

 What to do with all that time you save?

 The starkness and inevitability of death.

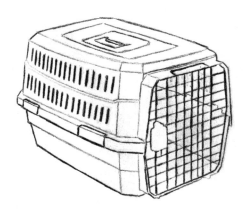

Mellors And The 'Wets'

'Everyone smiles in the same language.'

George Carlin

Even though Mellors is long gone as I write this, I still often feel the need to look over my shoulder should he be retraumatised as I relate the events of his harrowing day.

Now I am not saying Ingrid wasn't lovely. She was from 'Sveden' and I think this may have led to a few communication problems between us, but to be fair, she did her best.

Many vets had come and gone where Mellors was concerned – and some not without the scars to remind them of their encounter. The fact was that Mellors just did not like the vets.

On this occasion, I would not have taken him at all had it not been for the cattery who had a space for him over the few days I spent at my daughter's at Christmas who insisted he be vaccinated. An ordeal I had stopped putting him through long before for two reasons.

1. The sheer effort of catching him in a moment when he was in a reasonably good mood and actually

getting him into a carrying basket was more than I or he could bear. He seemed to develop six extra legs, none of which it seemed were in the basket at the same time during this procedure.

2. Secondly, there were few vets left in my hometown who were willing to risk their arms being torn to shreds. One had even placed a warning note on the surgery computer next to his name and recorded he was classed as a dangerous animal.

Here we were again in Rugby, along with Mellors' reputation and few vet practices left to choose from. I very much hoped the information on that wimpish vet's computer was kept confidential.

Of course, in my need to get him accommodated so that I did not have to spend Christmas alone, I was delighted to discover the relatively new practice and the unsuspecting Ingrid, and I may have been a little less than liberal with the truth as I hurriedly booked him in.

Preparations for 'the capture' started early that morning and I managed to escape with very few scratches considering his escape tactics had not diminished much over time. Eventually, we arrived at the surgery – Mellors had howled all the way in the car and snarled at the couple of dogs who approached his basket in the waiting room. I was flustered but determined now I was within a whisker's breadth of getting my longed-for holiday.

Ingrid asked if we had 'any problems with the vermin.' Mellors stopped shaking for a minute to look at me with disgust. "Yes," I said proudly, to ensure his hunting self-esteem remained intact, "Mellors catches loads of mice."

Then I realised she was asking me if he had been wormed. Not the most dignified of procedures at the best of times. Restrained in a towel, the administration of the tiny tablet – unbelievable how cats can hold this in their mouths for hours looking so angelic only to discover days later the now even tinier remnants of the medication under a chair. If on the rare occasion it does happen to be digested, the poor cat – not wanting to soil in the house – dives through the cat flap to evacuate explosively its entire stomach contents, hopefully along with the verms. (I recall a similar personal embarrassing experience on a bus in Tunisia several years ago minus cat flap and 'verms' when I had food poisoning.)

Ingrid, however, was not perturbed and determined to ensure Mellors got the full range of treatment the vets could offer. She donned some heavy duty gloves that went up to her elbows, grabbed the surprised Mellors and popped the pill in his mouth before he realised what was happening. She followed this with an even more undignified rectal examination, and if that wasn't enough, also administered the required vaccinations.

We left half an hour later. Mellors, having glanced at me in disbelief at allowing this violation, had voluntarily crawled sheepishly back into his carrier basket a damn sight quicker than it had taken me to get him in it earlier that morning. We drove home in silence. Mellors sulking because of his traumatic experience, me sulking because I now had gained a bill the size of a small mortgage.

Suffice to say, Mellors and the 'Wets' was never a match made in heaven. When we were recovering and I telephoned to pay the bill, the receptionist at the 'Wets' broke patient confidentiality and told me they had another cat on their books called Mellors! I never let on to the real Mellors – I didn't think it fair to burden him; he'd been through enough.

So, I was distracted for a while from my own worries and consumed with the importance of taking care of Mellors' health and happiness should he also 'leave me'. I was getting used to it being just the two of us again when something unexpected happened...

REFLECTIONS:
(FROM MELLORS - WHO DIDN'T SEE THE NEED
TO REFLECT MUCH)

 When the cat carrier basket appears, RUN and don't look back!

 Don't trust Swedish women wearing big gloves.

Reunited

'Fate brought you back
because our story
is not over yet.'

Anon

F riday 13th – I should have known. Not that I am superstitious – although I do recall another small driving incident that happened to take place on the date that strikes fear in some people's minds. I think it was probably more due to my lack of judgement and spatial awareness than the date, however, when I attempted to squeeze between a parked bus and a stationary car on the other side of the road. I didn't believe it possible (aside from in a comedy film) to get wedged between these two blameless vehicles – but wedged I was, with all three of us drivers almost holding our breath and wondering who was going to come off worst as I attempted to extricate myself from this embarrassing position. Needless to say, the bus (being the sturdiest vehicle) fared the best from my contact and I faced yet another hefty repair bill.

Driving back to my boat after a working trip, the almost spring evening had a freshness and increasing warmth. With the days becoming lighter, brighter and greener, I was in good spirits. Although still missing the

Labrador a lot, I was getting quite used to being alone on Argy (at least from a practical point of view) and felt proud of myself for surviving the winter alone. I was still not (and probably never will be) an expert navigator in the sense of squeezing through tight spaces and had many minor scrapes and cross looks from seasoned boaters on the short journeys needed to fetch water. However, 'necessity is the Mother of invention', as they say, and my innate resilience again served me well in the form of an outward false confidence. In any case, I still couldn't get back to my house in Winterton even if I had wanted to as court proceedings against my non-paying house guest seemed to be taking forever. A solicitor I had employed to evict him had messed up on the paperwork, adding at least another three months to my wait. I was also more than a little frustrated as I had gained a contract for some training work in the Norfolk area, meaning I had to pay to stay in a hotel when I visited, rather than my own house.

I was pondering on the unfairness of this and almost 'home' when my mobile phone rang. It was the Labrador! He said how much he had missed me and really wanted us to 'try again'. I wasn't aware I had stopped trying to make our relationship work – but again ignored my instincts and believed him to be right and me the bad person. Although I was getting used to being on my own, this newfound hope of a fairy tale ending soon washed over me and all fears of 'losing him' again melted away.

After a brief conversation (none of which shed any light on why he had decided to abandon me, where he had spent the last few months or indeed who with – with hindsight, quite important questions that I realise I was afraid to ask, not wanting to disrupt our relationship again), I made a further hasty decision and it was agreed

I would take my boat up to Braunston (approximately a three-hour cruise), where we would be reunited and sail back to Milton Keynes in romantic bliss together.

The café had barely reopened – the owners having an unexpected extended holiday beyond the planned February 1st – as I burst through the doors that evening to say I would shortly be leaving. They had made an exception for me and kindly let me moor up outside while they were away – not something that is usually allowed and I was anxious that I would have to move on when they got busy again. After the winter, the British Waterways warden would again be patrolling, notice that I had outstayed the normal two-week period allowed to boaters without a permanent mooring, and move me on. My stay had already been extended due to the particularly harsh wintry weather for a couple of weeks in January when the canal had been frozen and I couldn't have moved if I'd tried. So maybe it was fate, I pondered, that's why I had not got back to Winterton or moved from Rugby – we were meant to be together.

Mellors was grumpy – but then he was grumpy most days – maybe an age thing or he just had got tired of the disruptions and changes. His current lifestyle offered by the café owners suited him well. While I dined on way too much more wine than was good for me, he had enjoyed a bowl full of fish heads and the occasional lobster scraps. I was confident he would soon settle again wherever we were, and in any case, for once I was putting my happiness before his. I hardly slept with excitement that night.

It was very early the next morning, in preparation for my next big adventure, that I moved the few yards up the canal to the water point, filled up Argy's water tank and emptied the toilet. I couldn't believe what I was seeing as

I glanced through half-closed sleepy eyes and spotted the tail end of Mellors – clearly heading for another adventure of his own – precariously trotting across the closed lock gates to the other side of the canal. I shouted after him pointlessly and watched in despair as he disappeared into the fields beyond. Looking back, maybe he was trying to tell me he wanted to stay in Rugby. After all, it had been his home town too.

I was keen to move on though, so impatiently (and with a few sharp words and some meaty treats), I lured him back, carrying him precariously over my shoulder back across the lock gates. He clearly was having none of it. Digging his needle-like claws into my neck, he made his escape. I screamed in pain then watched in horror as he let out a loud miaow and, with a hopeless scramble to keep his footing, made a very undignified exit off the lock gate and into the canal.

Although cats can swim, they are not partial to getting wet, and Mellors was clearly no exception. Staring straight ahead, tail erect, fearfully struggling to keep his head above water as if he had just spent a fortune at the hairdresser, he presented a strange and unusual sight. He managed to swim quite quickly to the edge, which fortunately for him was not as high up as I had seen it in some parts of the canal. I was relieved I didn't have to go for a swim again to rescue him. One of the many dog owners I'd met had told me she had to save her small dog who had been in for a swim and couldn't get out again up the steep bank. I felt some sympathy for the now skinny looking drowned rat that was Mellors as I wrapped my sheepish companion in a towel and set off a little nervously for Braunston.

Reaching the middle lock at Hillmorton and glancing up at the towpath, I saw a couple of the locals who were waving me on my way. They had appeared quite aloof and kept themselves to themselves prior to this and any conversation had been on a limited social level. I did wonder what they thought of me – a woman alone on a small boat. Perhaps they were used to the transient nature of canal dwellers, not interested or even glad to see me go. Good job they were there though, as in my anxious state, I had completely forgotten how to work the locks! Unlike many gongoozlers, they were really helpful, and with a bit of verbal support and encouragement on this bright and fresh spring morning – a welcome reminder as to why I loved this boating life – I was soon on my way to retrieve what I thought would surely be my second chance of happiness.

Arriving in Braunston in good time, Mellors had almost dried off. Having regained my confidence, I decided to tackle the six locks there before the Labrador arrived. Manoeuvring Argy into the first lock, I was already looking forward to the celebratory glass of wine that would be awaiting us when we met at the canalside pub. The Admiral Nelson brought back happy childhood memories of warm summer days sitting outside with my parents, a bottle of ginger beer with a stripy paper straw and a packet of crisps containing the little blue waxed packet of salt you would shake in yourself. I had never imagined that the colourful passing boats that meandered past would one day play such a big part in my life and actually become my home.

Another boat decided to join me in the lock, and while chatting to the owner, I somehow managed to stall my engine. I turned the key to restart it and … nothing! No reassuring chug chug pop – the gentle sound that showed that Argy was fit and well.

The owner of the other boat, realising I was in trouble, helped by towing Argy out of the lock and to a safe place to moor on the bank. With amazing timing, I looked up after securing my boat with the ropes and saw the Labrador walking towards me on the towpath. He had moored the other side of the locks and watched from a distance as I was rescued. The passionate reunion I had dreamt of was beginning to look more and more distant as the Labrador, without even a glance at me, bounded over to jump on my boat and knelt down to peer into the gloomy depths of my bilges (the space at the lowest point between the floor of the engine room and the bottom of the boat). He stared at the defunct engine and worryingly shook his head.

"Oh Tillie – what have you done now?"

It was by then getting late and it seemed we would have to abandon all plans of getting to Milton Keynes that weekend. This was not a good start. My car was in Rugby, his in Milton Keynes. I was beginning to get that anxious feeling again. Having waited for this moment for months, now it felt like I was in danger of losing my independence once more. What if Argy was irreparable and I had to live on his boat again – surely that would not help to repair our relationship?

Saturday dawned. We had spent the previous evening – what was left of it – on his boat talking about what to do. I was so pleased to see him but it felt like the grand reunion had been spoilt by this unexpected hitch and practical matters took priority. Whatever happened, I hoped we could get back to some sort of normal and that he was equally as pleased to see me. Though I had a tiny fear that his normal might not have been the same as mine and I was not quite so important to him. I wondered if he had sensed the newfound confidence I had acquired while living alone for all those months. What if not being dependent on him had changed his feelings towards me?

We walked along to the local boatyard and spoke to the mechanic, who was more than willing to take a look – amazingly, he was the very person who had, a few years ago, serviced the engine in Argy. Over an hour or so, he lovingly did whatever it is you do to resuscitate dead boats and then we were on our way – and not too much behind schedule.

We had a wonderful sunny cruise to Milton Keynes, arriving earlier than expected. Mellors settled very quickly this time and would not stop purring. The Labrador seemed to think it was because he was pleased to see him but I sensed it was probably due to him having devoured almost an entire chicken that the Labrador had cooked for him. I think, looking back, the Labrador was attempting to 'buy' the affection that Mellors showed to me and possibly even isolate me from him.

I still had no knowledge of where the Labrador had been and I felt it best not to ask. It seemed less risky to our future happiness to try to forget the last few months. This was made easier by the improved living conditions – lots of facilities, great shopping, easy car parking and so many green, open spaces. I had forgotten quite how beautiful it was there.

We soon got back to being more settled and it started to feel like it had when we first met. However, we had barely been back at Giffard Park a week when he had to go away for work – this time to Berlin. I had never visited Berlin so we agreed I would go too, at least for half the trip, as I had to be back in the UK for work before his trip ended.

I saw very little of this culturally rich city, having spent the first couple of days with the Labrador (who was photographing at a trade conference), not wanting to let him far out of my sight given his habit of disappearing. It was rather strange staying in a hotel. Although I made good use of the refreshing shower there, I was beginning to lose the desire for such luxurious living.

On my last day in Berlin, I visited the Jewish Museum – an experience that will stay with me forever. Aside from the incredible stark architecture of Daniel Libeskind and moving photographs of this tragic time in history, the whole experience attempted to replicate what it must have been like for the European Jews driven from their homes during the Second World War. The Garden of Exile is particularly disorientating. As you walk through the rows of concrete pillars, you get a sense of not knowing which path to choose or whether to stay or go.

I returned to England after a few days with more than a few reservations about leaving the Labrador. Quickly trying to erase these from my mind, I focussed on my journey, marvelling at the efficiency and cleanliness of the German train that took me to the airport.

As I walked along the towpath towards the spot where our boats were moored, I looked at the Labrador's boat from a distance and noticed she seemed to be moored at a strange angle – the front end being much higher than the back. I wondered for a moment if my brain was confused as I was tired and my few days spent in Berlin and off my boat had not been enough to fully restore my land legs. *Mal de debarquement* – translated as 'illness of disembarkment' – is an interesting condition that I was quite unprepared for. It is a strange sensation as the body and brain adjust to the motion of the boat and causes actual sea sickness in the extreme. However, the dizziness, unsteadiness and wobbly legs is not noticeable until you venture onto dry land. The first time I experienced the weird swaying feeling when being off my boat for a few days, I wondered what was happening.

The only other time I had spent any length of time on a boat was on a school cruise holiday at twelve years old, where the ship's turbulence as we sailed through the Bay of Biscay caused most passengers, crew and even the captain to be seasick. Surprisingly, given my normally weak stomach, I did not experience any such reaction.

As I curiously approached the boat, confused at what I was seeing, I heard a loud hissing sound. On further cautious investigation, I realised it was coming from the water tank. Now, even with my limited technical knowledge, it seemed to me that to make this sound the tank must be empty. I went onto the boat, turned on the tap in the sink and confirmed my diagnosis. As I could hear the pump still running, I could only assume that someone – and I am not religious, but at that moment I prayed it wasn't me – had left the tap on and drained the tank. This in itself would not have been serious, and had I gone no further onto the boat at that point, I would not have discovered that the kitchen and shower room floor was ankle deep in water. I stood looking down as various interesting items floated around my feet – a few slices of bread, some Oxo cubes and a lump of cheese all seemed strangely out of context, adding to my confusion, and I started to panic – the boat was surely sinking. I tried a couple of times to phone the Labrador but he must have had his phone switched off.

In my mind, there was no time to waste. Grabbing the

biggest saucepan I could find – which, to be fair, wasn't very big – I started to bail out, stopping only for a few minutes as I heard another boat passing. I scrambled above deck, slipping and sliding on the wet and quite muddy floor to shout for help. Help came in the form of a suggestion from a seemingly unperturbed boater who recommended soaking up the water with disposable nappies. He generously threw me a couple of spares he happened to have aboard! Once I had used them (they barely had any impact on the swirling muddy pool), I rushed out to the supermarket and bought the biggest pack I could afford.

I can only assume babies do not excrete the volume of liquid that required absorption here. However, three hours and a very achy arm later, the nappies and the saucepan had enabled me to get the water level down to around one inch deep. By now, it was getting dark as I sat back and surveyed the scene, worried that I had not done enough and that the Labrador would think me hopeless. Gradually calming down, I noticed the boat had reached a more level angle and the water level was no longer rising. I realised I could do little more, considering with relief that the boat was not sinking but there had probably been a pipe leaking underneath the floor. Now that the tank was empty, I realised that any further effort on my part was probably not worth making. I may as well wait for the Labrador to come home and start up the bilge pump to get rid of the remaining water below.

Retiring to my boat exhausted and feeling satisfied with my management of this 'emergency' (although rather foolish for imagining the worst), I was now really looking forward to the Labrador coming home.

When he arrived a couple of days later, he seemed pleased when I related to him what I had done.

"You are an amazing woman – you have saved my boat. Maybe I should marry you."

REFLECTIONS:

 You have the right to be angry with someone you love.

 It is almost impossible to think clearly when in a panic.

 Carl Jung said, "Until you make the unconscious conscious, it will direct your life and you will call it Fate." I have spent much of my life ignoring these wise words.

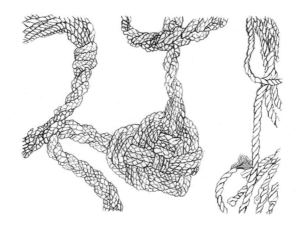

Ring Of
Bright Water

'He has married me with a ring, a ring of bright water
Whose ripples travel from the heart of the sea,
He has married me with a ring of light, the glitter
Broadcast on the swift river.'

Kathleen Raine (The Marriage of Psyche)

t had never entered my thoughts that I would get married again. However, it wasn't long (as with my other hastily thought through decisions) before I became swept away with the delights of making plans. It felt like the Labrador also wanted to have the perfect wedding.

Firstly, the exciting shopping tips to choose the engagement ring – eventually purchased from a tiny antique shop in Amersham, a quaint town in Buckinghamshire. It was a delicate vintage marcasite and diamond ring – not expensive and understated – reflecting my feeling of not quite being sure of myself in believing this was actually happening to me. Then followed the 'official' proposal, which took place over a romantic dinner in the same town. It all felt like a bit of a dream and somehow like he was following the protocol without much feeling. It crossed my mind that he may have been quite practised in these rituals. I never had the courage to question how his past relationships had ended, although I believed there had been quite a few since his marriage – a time which he also spoke little of apart from saying he was very much the injured party and his wife was abusive to him.

He did speak of one woman who he had worked with and they began an affair. He said she had become 'too needy'. I don't recall quite where we were moored at the time, but it was early on in our relationship when we were walking along the towpath near his boat when a woman walking the other way said hello to him. He looked shocked to see her and I realised this was her. She seemed perfectly OK to me – she said she was walking in the area and had spotted his boat so she thought she'd come and say hello. She was very chatty about how pleased she was to see him and I invited her back to the boat for a coffee. I have to admit, I was hoping to find something out about his past but she didn't give much away. He didn't speak much either – in fact, I think he was glad when she left.

Any doubts that arose again were held firmly in the back of my mind as we continued to plan our 'perfect' wedding.

There is little information about what happened historically at weddings of canal dwellers. All Saint's Church is in Braunston village – which lies at the junction of the Grand Union and Oxford Canal – and is known as the cathedral of the canals. It is said that passing boatmen might have met and married local girls and set up home in the village. It is thought there would have also been lively and colourful unofficial ceremonies, likely not to have taken place in church but on the boats themselves.

Traditions such as handfasting (where the bride and groom's hands were tied together with a handkerchief or scarf) and 'jumping the broomstick', to symbolise a new beginning and to sweep away the past, signified the couple were unofficially bound in marriage. I'm imagining the broomstick might have been replaced with 'leaping the bargepole'.

Neither of us had any religious beliefs so we settled for a hotel ceremony in Rugby, although it was by the water in a sense as, set in the countryside, it overlooked the beautiful Draycote reservoir.

In the middle of us making our plans came another work trip away for the Labrador – this time to Poland. I was feeling more secure about spending more time together following his unexpected marriage proposal and even imagined we might get a bigger boat and live together again. After all, he surely wouldn't have asked me to marry him if he didn't want this too? I decided to go to Poland with him as I didn't want to spend time on my own much anymore.

Looking back, I think what followed was probably the beginning of the end of our relationship. As we were in the taxi travelling to the airport, I started to develop a sharp pain in my neck and shoulder. I thought at first it might have been caused by sitting in a draught from my mainly uninsulated boat but it got worse and worse, and by the time we arrived at the hotel in Poland, I could barely move and spent the rest of the day and all night lying on the bed. The Labrador had arranged to meet some colleagues for a meal and I just couldn't face that so he went alone.

I could only remember a little of the French I had learned at school and the Labrador, even more disadvantaged, only knew English – both of little use there. However, somehow the next morning we managed to overcome the language barrier with the Polish speaking hotel receptionist and gesticulate rather dramatically that we needed to find a doctor.

I was just beginning to wish I'd brought my trusty Rhoda as he directed us to a clinic. However, it fortunately happened to be just around the corner from the hotel. I was very sceptical about the quality of the care they might offer in this unknown country on a Saturday morning, but to be honest, by that time I would have let them amputate my arm if it would have taken the pain away.

We were directed by a nurse at the entrance – I had no idea if she had grasped from my poor sign language why we were there – to wait in a sparsely furnished but spotlessly clean huge waiting area. Around the outside were a number of doors with nameplates – all in Polish. There were a couple of children crying and clinging to their mothers and several older people among the seemingly growing crowd of patients all waiting to be seen. I felt anxious and hoped they had understood from my sign language accompanied by words spoken in a pseudo Polish accent why I was there.

After two hours or so, one of the doors opened and I was called in. A very handsome and extremely tall doctor – well, I assumed he was a doctor as he wore a white coat – to my relief spoke enough English to establish what was wrong. He carefully examined my what I now know was a 'frozen shoulder' and gave me a slip of paper directing us back to the reception desk where we had come in. Here, I was given a packet of tablets (directions in Polish) along with another slip of paper – this time clearly a bill for about 235 Polish Zloty (around £50).

The following day, after risking what I thought might have been an appropriate number of tablets at various intervals during the night, I felt no better. We returned to the clinic, thinking they would surely be closed on a

Sunday morning, but no, they seemed busier than ever. The Labrador was his usual chatty and confident self, introducing me as if I were a small child. He appeared very caring as he struck up a conversation with a waiting patient who spoke very clear English. She explained that behind each of the eight or so doors in the clinic was a consultant with a different speciality. I had been lucky enough to see one of the best orthopaedic consultants in the area. I felt more confident to go back in with this knowledge. This time, I was given an injection into my shoulder, which managed to get me through the rest of the week with much less pain. We went to the reception desk on the way out expecting to pay more money. Instead, we were surprised to receive all of our money back as the medication hadn't helped! I pondered on how long it might take to see any consultant back in the UK, especially for free.

We managed to enjoy the remainder of the week with the Labrador working and me doing a little sightseeing, alternating with reading in the hotel room during the day. In the evenings, we would go out for a meal with his colleagues. I began again to experience that slight feeling of unease as my partial incapacity seemed to irritate the Labrador, especially when we were with his colleagues, when he liked to be the centre of attention.

When we had first met, he liked to 'show me off'. I'm guessing he didn't like to show what he saw as the flaws in me when I was not looking or feeling my best. He was a very 'big' character when with others, talking a lot and very impressive with his achievements. Women seemed to love him – hanging on his every word. I often blended into the background on these occasions – not feeling like I had much to share or talk about that would interest them.

On our return home, things between us seemed OK again. We had lots of discussions about the wedding plans and started to draft a guest list. My side was easy, but when it came to discussing his family we seemed to hit another barrier. I had met his two teenage sons as they had visited the boat many times, often camping out in the woods alongside the towpath. I knew he had a daughter too, and a granddaughter of about three years old who he barely mentioned. I pushed him a little, saying it would be good if she could come to the wedding and he got angry, saying he hadn't spoken to her for some time following what seemed to me like a very trivial argument. He had never met his granddaughter. I thought of my own family – of course, we have had our disagreements, but to cut them out of my life completely seemed harsh and unimaginable.

We were invited to London's China Town for a special dinner by one of the Labrador's clients and his family. The meal was an authentic Chinese cuisine, and believe me, it was nothing like the number 47 with fried rice that I had previously enjoyed from my local takeaway. I did not realise there were so many different ways of cooking and serving squid – at least, I think it was squid but I couldn't be sure. The Labrador, of course, consumed everything in front of him with relish and kept glaring at me and whispering that it was considered rude to his clients to refuse these delicacies.

By the time we got to the high spot of the meal, when they brought out a small plate of duck's tongues, I had consumed rather a lot of red wine in an attempt to both aid digestion and disguise the taste of what I was swallowing. The wine also helped me to dissociate from my discomfort of not feeling I fitted in as the Labrador's 'guest'. I amused myself by pondering why, of all the ducks

I had seen on the canal, I had never noticed whether they had tongues. However, I was aware that ducks have no teeth so they would never have to experience the pain of biting their tongues. Somehow, I was finding I might have to learn to metaphorically bite mine more often when in the Labrador's company.

REFLECTIONS:

 I am not responsible for others' behaviour, feelings, or problems.

 There is no need to apologise for being you.

 It is OK to terminate conversations with people, if you feel put down or humiliated.

Comedy Or
Tragedy?

'Am I in Earth, in heaven,
or in hell?
Sleeping or waking, mad
or well-advised?
Known unto these, and
to myself disguised?
I'll say as they say, and
persever so,
And in this mist at all
adventures go.'

William Shakespeare (*The Comedy of Errors*)

We continued to be very busy over the next few weeks, making plans and talking about who we might invite to the wedding. I was still keen to establish a reunion between the Labrador and his daughter and hoped I would get to know her better. Perhaps she could provide me with a little more sense of his past, which was still very vague. This vagueness worried me, considering I was about to spend the rest of my life with someone – more than likely on his home ground.

Eventually, he agreed to us visiting her on the condition that we enjoyed a cruise and moved our boats up towards West London, nearer to where she and his boys lived. A short journey took us back to moor our boats near Berkhamsted.

When we met his daughter, she seemed very natural and friendly, and I could get no understanding of what she could possibly have done to upset him so much. She did once disclose to me how hurt she had felt when he 'cut her out' but she didn't seem to have any idea why she had fallen out of favour with him any more than I did.

I was feeling we were certainly a long way from Rugby now. However, the Labrador was still great fun to be with at times, just as he had been at the beginning of our relationship, and we enjoyed much in common – the same sense of humour, the same music and we laughed a lot. Nevertheless, his sudden and unexplained descents into dark moods (to which I nearly always felt guilt for contributing to) often ended in his drinking to unconsciousness, scaring me, and were becoming more frequent and unpredictable.

On a social level, we were still functioning as a loving couple – still holding hands in public, laughing together – but underneath, I felt things were slowly crumbling, although no one seemed to notice.

We visited The Globe Theatre on the South Bank, as I had been given two tickets – as part of my leaving present from my previous job in Norfolk – to see the Shakespeare play, *The Comedy of Errors*. I had seen a couple of Shakespeare plays in Stratford-upon-Avon many years before, but seeing one in this venue was a different, confusing-to-the-brain experience – the contrast of being immersed in the era of the play disrupted by planes frequently flying overhead, as the Globe has no roof.

We had both found more work – the Labrador at a large advertising agency and me teaching at a local college. I was enjoying the variety of my working life and was still offering training courses in care homes all over the UK.

We often worked late into the evening so didn't do a lot of cooking on board, although I had bought a lovely little book of favourite boating recipes. There was certainly plenty of food around to use in these recipes in the hedgerows and areas around the towpaths. We would forage mushrooms, apples and blackberries. Some of the recipes in the book had names such as Lock-keeper's Casserole, which would have made use of some of this 'free' food and anything else available, such as fresh watercress growing by the water's edge, and wild rabbit – although I could never have brought myself to catch and kill one, but I'm sure the Labrador would have. (Some months into our life together, I discovered that he kept an air rifle hidden in the back of a cupboard on his boat, which unnerved me more than a little.)

The Lock-Keepers cottages we came across often had small gardens attached where fruit and vegetables flourished. Of course, there would be plenty of fish, eels and ducks available too – the ducks hopefully with their tongues intact.

Talking of gardens reminds me of the time we visited a couple in their late fifties – acquaintances of the Labrador – who lived on a wide beam boat. I'll just say somewhere in Hertfordshire.

As we approached their boat, the familiar smell of cannabis (reminding me of Notting Hill Carnival) was prevalent in a low mist around it. George, clearly stoned even though it was only 10am, staggered a little unsteadily towards us. I learned later from the Labrador that this was George's permanent state, having usually smoked at least three joints before breakfast time. Breakfast for him consisted of a whisky – although he did say he was trying not to drink much, having been lucky enough to survive a liver transplant the previous year. A wiry man, ex-navy, his clothes reminiscent of the sixties hippy era, with suede waistcoat, flowery tunic and denim jeans, topped with a wide brimmed leather boater's hat.

He was pleased to see us and eager to show us his 'garden'. Apparently, he had purchased himself an unofficial title of Lord along with a fairly large patch of land at the end of a small path hidden from the towpath by overhanging trees. It took me a while to realise what the prolific green crops were that George was so proud to show us. Suffice to say there was enough of them to keep the population of Hertfordshire in a very happy mood for a very long time.

After suitably expressing our admiration for his work, we went to their boat to meet his wife, Anne. It was like stepping into a small cottage, twice the size of our two boats put together, beautifully and comfortably furnished, cosy and inviting with a proper shower room, flushing toilet, two bedrooms complete with built-in full size fitted wardrobes. I was quite envious and made a mental note to discuss the possibility of us owning a boat like this when we were married. Anne had a homely relaxed air about her too, wearing a flowery apron that was protecting a long gathered skirt and white lacy loose blouse barely concealing her ample (and from what I could see) braless bosoms. She was clearly immersed in a very big cake baking session, I deduced from the delicious smell that was coming from the Aga. After offering us a glass of whisky – which I declined and the Labrador accepted – she paused only to make me a cup of tea.

They were such a fascinating and intelligent couple and I enjoyed their conversation, which was mainly around how they got together as a couple, first living on dry land having met in London in the sixties when George had 'left' the Navy, and then moving onto their own boat, living this freer lifestyle and staking their claim to their piece of the countryside alongside their boat. I listened in amazement to George as he described his alcoholism and subsequent life-saving liver transplant and much other surgery which seemed to have related to removal or replacement of most of his bodily organs at one time or another. As with many 'addicts', he seemed almost indestructible, having survived the most unimaginable (albeit self-imposed) traumas. I imagined Anne had tolerated much from him during their time together too, although they seemed to be a happy, loving and contented couple, treating each other with care and respect.

This was the first time anyone had talked to me about the Labrador's previous long term girlfriend – who they had clearly liked and met many times – questioning openly why the relationship had ended. Again, there was no clear answer from the Labrador, aside from the fact that she had 'moved on'.

As we were talking (and after I eventually had succumbed to a small glass of whisky – which I can't bear the taste of, by the way), there was a knock on the door of their boat. Looking out of the window, I was a little worried – given the boat was now slowly refilling with a cannabis haze and bearing in mind the contents of their garden – to see three uniformed policemen. I was surprised when Anne and George didn't look worried and even more astonished when Anne produced a couple of cardboard cake boxes from one of the kitchen cupboards, filled them with the cakes she had just removed from the oven, and handed them out through the hatches to the waiting officers. Noticing I looked a bit concerned, she gave me a wink and a half smile and simply said, "They always come for their orders around this time."

As we left, George filled two plastic carrier bags with more of his fresh produce for our leaving present. As we walked back the short distance to where our boats were moored, I hoped that it might help us to enjoy the happy, carefree relationship and lifestyle that they seemed to have and we had once enjoyed – although there was a little voice getting louder in my head that I still wasn't ready to listen to … and I noticed we weren't holding hands as we used to.

REFLECTIONS:

 Feelings can be triggered. However, it is not possible to 'make' someone feel a certain emotion – that is their choice.

 Treat with caution people who constantly speak badly of others, are estranged from their family, or if you have not met their friends.

 There are many creative ideas for presents.

The End

'If a cat does something, we call it instinct; if we do the same thing, for the same reason, we call it intelligence.'

Will Cuppy

I t was one of those evenings where we decided we didn't want to cook so we had walked to the pub just off the towpath. As usual, Mellors – not wanting to be left out – had followed us.

The pub was a large modern one with one open plan dining area and was particularly busy on that night. We managed to get a table in the middle of the room – not something I am particularly comfortable with, preferring to sit by the window. Mellors usually gave up when he saw us enter the pub and went back to the boat or did whatever might occupy him in the surrounding fields until we returned home. We were mid wedding plan conversation when I looked up to see Mellors stroll into the pub and head towards our table.

The couple at the next table were already glaring at me and did not seem to be as amused as we were. A waitress was fast heading towards us, mumbling about health and hygiene rules and that she would have to call the police if we did not remove him. Tempting though it was to see what the police may have said to being called out on a no doubt busy Friday night in London to remove this 'dangerous animal', we decided to follow the rules. We had ordered our food by this stage and were quite hungry. I took Mellors back to the boat with a few choice words and placed him firmly in the well deck. We continued with our meal.

Mellors returned and was sitting by the glass door of the pub, looking longingly through it at us and trying to sneak in with every customer that came in or out of the door. He was becoming quite a celebrity, much to the annoyance of the waitress. Our evening was interrupted further by us taking out pieces of chicken for him from time to time just to show there were no hard feelings. I did think it was strange behaviour for him and wondered what he was trying to tell me. I often got a sense that he understood me, especially when I was upset or worried about something.

When we left the pub that evening, he was strutting proudly around the car park being further admired by quite a crowd of people, getting much sympathy and fuss. Even though he'd probably eaten more chicken than we had that evening, he played the starving homeless cat role very convincingly and gained much sympathy with many exclamations of "Ooh" and "Ah" and "Poor thing!"

We were still deep in conversation as we walked back to our boats and I assumed he had followed us home. However, he didn't come home that night ... or the next, or the next.

I was distraught. I couldn't bear the thought of losing him – he had been my companion and ally through all the traumas of the last few years. We searched and searched. We pinned notices with his photo (of which we had many) onto trees along the towpath. We trawled the streets surrounding the canal – or at least I did this alone after the first few days, when the Labrador got bored with the idea. His initial support in the search, I felt, was more about him looking good and appearing to care about Mellors' disappearance. I wondered if he was secretly pleased that he now may be free of competition for my affection. I was reluctant to move our boats again in case he came back and we had a couple of discussions about this as I knew that the Labrador wouldn't want to stay in one place for long. He was planning to move even nearer to his family and further from mine, I sensed.

It was around a month later and two months before our wedding and I had almost given up all hope of finding Mellors. I was standing in the queue to pay for petrol at the garage when my mobile phone rang. A woman's voice said, "Have you lost a cat? I think we may have him here." Mumbling my apologies about 'an emergency' to everyone who got in my way as I pushed to the front of the queue, I threw down my money at the till to pay for the petrol and jumped into my car, relieved to find that Rhoda was on top form and clearly showed the house was only about a ten-minute drive.

As I walked up the path to the house, I couldn't help noticing it was not dissimilar to my house in Winterton. Excitement mixed with anxiety in anticipation of either being united with my trusty friend or this being a case of mistaken identity (a Mellors lookalike) must have contributed to me looking a rather emotional and dishevelled mess when the woman answered the door. She looked at me rather suspiciously, I thought. Then, over her shoulder in the lounge, I spotted him. He was curled up and gently washing himself in a beautiful wicker cat basket, not unlike the expensive one I had purchased for him at home – the same one that he flatly refused to go anywhere near, and in the end, I gave away to the charity shop. In that moment, I forgave him all of that, and near to tears, I called out to him. He looked up. I thought for a moment he recognised me, then he turned his back on me and continued with his wash. The woman looked at me even more suspiciously as if I were some evil cat thief. She asked what I wanted to do as she was unable to give Mellors a permanent home as she had a dog who currently was having to be kept in the shed to keep them apart. (I could hardly hide a smile when I heard that Mellors had already taken a swipe at him).

"Of course I'll take him home," I said, thanking her for her trouble.

I picked up Mellors, ignoring his feeble attempt at a meow, and bundled him into the car. I'm sure I saw him wink at me.

Every time I left my boat after that, even for a short time, I made sure it was securely locked with Mellors on the inside. Although he never made another bid for freedom, I can't help thinking he had enjoyed what turned out to be his final adventure. I didn't realise it was shortly to be the end of mine too.

There were only weeks to go to the wedding – guests had been invited (including the Labrador's daughter), deposits paid, menu decided. We sat outside our other local pub, basking in the sunshine one afternoon, talking about some last minute details. I was to travel to Norfolk early the following morning to deliver a training course – ironically, it turned out, on abuse. The Labrador seemed distracted and spent most of the time looking into the distance behind me at a woman who was sitting at another table. Eventually, I got irritated by this and told him so. Without speaking, he got up and walked back to his boat. I followed to try to reason with him but he had locked himself in. That's where he remained.

Later that evening, I tried again and he unlocked his door. After a distressing argument, I suggested we leave it until we had both calmed down and talk when I got back from Norfolk. I was anything but calm as I drove there at 5am the next morning, having had a disturbed night with only snatches of sleep. We were used to messaging each other regularly when working, often several times a day. He did not respond to my messages and voicemails that day. I don't know how I got through the delivery of the course, which was difficult enough in any case due to the subject matter – now even more upsetting.

I eventually got back to my boat at around 10pm that evening and the space where his boat was moored next to mine was taken by a different boat. I was tired and confused and could not really take in what I was seeing. I called him several times and still no response.

After a few days of trying, I realised I had to give up. Cancelling the wedding arrangements and letting people know was difficult – hence it is a bit vague now as I dissociated from my feelings and focussed on essential tasks. I was grateful for being able to do most of this via emails rather than having to speak to people in person. It all felt too painful.

REFLECTIONS:

 Never trust a man who doesn't like cats. I understand this as someone who can't tolerate the other's independence – this is not good in a human relationship.

 You don't need to suffer in silence – it's fine to tell anyone you wish how unhappy you are, and strength is shown not by coping alone but instead by asking for emotional support.

 I have the right to grieve over what I didn't get that I needed, or what I got that I didn't need or want.

Sailing By

'I'll do my crying
in the rain.'

Howard Greenfield

tried really hard to get back on my feet. I couldn't face the thought of being alone again. It was a little easier while the weather was good but the idea of getting through another lone winter on my boat felt too much to contemplate.

For a few months, I sat with my despair and spent much time alone, fixated on the thought he might come back as he had the last time. Mellors was consistently contented and seemed to be happy he now had me to himself.

I continued to work in various short term contracts in London and Norfolk. The turning point came – as it often does – when I had reached 'rock bottom'. I had been working in Hammersmith and had finished earlier than expected, so with a sudden impulsive burst of optimism and a desperate need for some self-care, I decided to travel to Brick Lane – one of my favourite places and where Rankin (my photographer hero who I often tried to emulate with my own images) was exhibiting his work. Of course, nothing is straightforward for me – especially, it seems, when I have spontaneous ideas.

Getting off at Aldgate East Station, a five-minute walk away from the Truman Brewery where the exhibition was held, the sky darkened and the heavens opened. Within two minutes, I was completely soaked through. Undeterred, I squelched around, taking in the amazing exhibition – what I could see of it through my fogged-up specs – leaving a trail of water behind me like an incontinent slug. The reception staff were as helpful as they could be, directing me to the toilets where there were a couple of paper towels. However, my efforts to mop up were futile, given the quantity of water that had soaked through every item of clothing I was wearing, including at least a pint that had collected in my bra.

Fearing pneumonia was setting in and still having a half hour journey on the tube back to my car in my new wet look clothes, I didn't stay long. Surprisingly for that time of the evening, tube travellers seemed to be keeping their distance and I even got a seat to myself with lots of space around it.

By the time I got to the car, I knew I could not face the hour or so drive in wet clothes. To add to my misery, the toilets near the car park were closed so I couldn't change into the spare set I had in the car. Foolishly, I thought I could get away with changing in the car park lift if I kept my finger on the door close button. Had I known there were a group of stag night revellers heading for the lift, making an early start to their evening, I may have thought of a different plan. Still, at least I managed to change my skirt before they got on. My top was changed quickly and discretely in my car after moving the vehicle to a corner away from the security camera. Proud of my resourceful efforts and determination, I laughed to myself – yet another scrape I had got myself through alone. Smiling inwardly, I pondered if it could have been worse – my photographer hero, Rankin, could have been there in person and captured my soggy state on camera. Regaining my humour was a positive sign for me that I could get through this.

As I walked back along the towpath to my boat that summer evening, I noticed in the distance there was the biggest, brightest, brilliant rainbow above it. This surely was another sign of hope for me and the beginning of accepting the reality – this was indeed the end of what had been a toxic relationship.

This time I had learnt to plan my recovery a little more strategically, so I launched myself into practical issues and securing my future – even though I wasn't sure what that held for me.

My first step was to reclaim my house in Winterton. I contacted my solicitor there – I'm convinced solicitors do nothing unless you persist in ringing them – and discovered that as all other avenues had been exhausted, there was only one alternative left to eject my shifty tenant. Plans were set to send in the bailiffs the following week. I really wanted to be there to see the moment he was evicted but as it turned out, it was a bit of a non event as my neighbour had reported he had been seen leaving early that morning.

I decided to find a myself a therapist to work on the grief I was experiencing. I had previously had some counselling many years earlier, which I found helpful when going through a difficult emotional trauma. So much so, it inspired me to pursue my own counselling training and I qualified with an Advanced Diploma – although I hadn't put my skills into practice much, apart from teaching on counselling courses and some voluntary work with charities.

I found a therapist in London and I spent the three sessions I had with him mostly crying. It was such a relief to be able to offload to someone. Although I didn't get much further than this with him, it was all helping me to process and grieve for my losses past and present. I also was aware that I would shortly be leaving this therapeutic relationship behind me as I moved back to my house. I think this helped me to be able to talk about what I felt more openly as I believed I would never come across this 'listening ear' again. In fact, I did a lot of crying in the next few weeks, although once I had made my decisions, it was clear there was little time to be spent on my emotions – I just had to do this!

The other thing I needed to do was to sell Argy. I realised I had little more idea how to go about this than I'd had when I bought him. I spoke to a couple of people moored nearby and they suggested selling him privately with a word of warning to beware of people turning up with cash and pressurising me to sell on the spot. However, given my experience of letting my house, I was thinking more clearly and decided to ring around some boatyards to see if they would take care of the sale for me. Of course, this meant I may lose money on the sale as they would be taking commission, but this seemed a small price to pay for my peace of mind. I was still feeling quite vulnerable and wanted to make this difficult process as easy as possible.

I found the nearest yard willing to take on the sale was in Leighton Buzzard – around a four to five-hour cruise away – and I decided to move there so the handover could go more smoothly. An added advantage was that I wouldn't have to wait around once Argy had been handed over, so I first moved my car there and travelled back to Argy by taxi.

I sensed I was going to miss the tiny protective shell that had been my home for those last few years.

As I prepared to move Argy to his final (for the moment) resting place, true to form, he put up a fight to the last. It was a very windy day, but that does not come close to explaining how, when I untied the ropes, Argy did an extremely swift turn around and started to head off in the opposite direction, leaving me hanging on to the rope for dear life, my feet getting nearer and nearer the edge of the cut, sliding rapidly through the mud as if in a losing tug o'war team. I managed to hang on, however – it is surprising what strength you can muster in a crisis. Shouting a few words (not for publication), I leapt on his rear end like a seasoned rodeo rider, took control of the tiller for the last time, and promptly burst into tears.

Those last few weeks had taken their toll on my emotions and I don't think I realised quite how much I would miss not only his security but also his cheeky character.

As I started to pack, I gazed out of Argy's small porthole onto the water, enjoying the reflections of the red and gold leaves in what was left of the autumn sunlight. I felt sad as I reminisced over some of the memories I had gathered over our years together. I came across the penknife with all the twiddly bits – probably for getting stones out of horse's hooves, as my dad used to joke. My eldest daughter had finally settled on this thoughtful and practical Christmas present in place of the hairdryer she had originally suggested. Never the need to use it on a horse, it came in very handy at the time when my only corkscrew broke while attempting to open my last bottle of Shiraz as I was desperate to gain its comforting warmth. And where did all these coat hangers come from? It is a well-known fact that they breed in wardrobes and I think my boat must have been a particularly fertile place as they seemed to outnumber any clothes worthy of hanging by at least two to one. I found the hairbrush – hardly used since I'd been living on the boat. Packed originally to use with my now defunct hair straighteners in my mistaken belief that I would be able to style my hair and maintain some sort of neat appearance rather than the dishevelled one I only ever seemed able to achieve in those later months. As I idly ran it through my hair, a rather large dead spider fell onto my lap – I had no idea how long it had been there!

My peace was disturbed by the sound of splashing, shouting and cheering gradually getting louder and causing me to look out of the hatch. The sounds came from an approaching canoe, part of a race led by a team of strong women rowing for their lives. I knew I would need all my strength over the coming weeks and months as I made my transition to my previous life.

It was the coldest day of the year when my youngest daughter, granddaughter in tow, made the long journey from Leeds to collect the bulk of my belongings to take back to Winterton.

I cried again when she arrived. I was so grateful for her being there and I knew how difficult it was for her to find the time, with a small and newish baby. She waited patiently while I laboriously finished my packing – cherishing every item. I didn't want to leave any part of me on Argy and I was amazed, having loaded her car up to the roof, with how the few possessions I had originally brought to my new life had seemingly expanded into a houseful again. Then I set about loading my car with an almost equal amount.

My daughter set off for Norfolk with my beautiful and equally patient granddaughter safely strapped into her child seat – although looking nervously at the massive towers of saucepans, clothes and books that surrounded her.

After taking Argy's keys to the boatyard, I returned to stand by him for a few minutes. As I whispered my goodbyes, a familiar looking boat caught my eye. I couldn't believe what I was seeing as the Labrador sailed past, giving me a wave and a smile as he would have done to any stranger passing by. I was stunned and knew then there was nothing more to do or say. I got into my car and drove home.

REFLECTIONS:

 There is no such thing as waterproof mascara, apart from when you actually want to remove it when it suddenly takes on an indelible quality.

 The therapeutic relationship is more important than the content of the therapy work.

Driving Home
For Christmas

'... with a thousand memories.'

Chris Rea

t was dark and Winterton-on-Sea village was looking lovely with a huge Christmas tree aglow on the green as I drove past and through the narrow street that led to my cottage. Everywhere I looked, there were houses probably unashamedly using a year's supply of electricity in one evening, with colourful twinkling lights, snowmen, reindeers and Santas.

I was anxious as to what I might find as I walked through the front door and relieved to see that on first inspection my home was still in one piece with no obvious damage inflicted by my wayward tenant from hell. I slept surprisingly well on my first night, even without the rocking of my boat to lull me to sleep. (I was to experience the unsteadiness of my land legs for some weeks to come though).

A week or so later, Mellors – traumas from his boating life far behind him now – sniffed expectantly at the pan containing the ham I was cooking in preparation for some pre-Christmas visitors. He looked up at me, hopeful I may accidentally drop a morsel of meat for him to devour. He never ceased to amaze me, how quickly he adapted to his new surroundings, and had not stopped purring since we arrived. He took up his place in the window, watching and waiting for his old enemy, Skimble, the cat next door, to appear. Their relationship, as with most of Mellors' relationships, was always more than a little troubled. From the bedroom window, I would see Skimble creeping stealthily and deliberately on his side of the dividing garden wall, oblivious to the fact that Mellors would be doing the same on my side. My neighbour and I would leap outside, hosepipes primed, waiting for the two opponents to notice each other when they reached the gap in the wall at the bottom of the gardens and fur would start to fly. I made a mental note to dig out the hosepipe from the shed to prepare for the next bout.

Village life seemed to be going on as if I had never been away. No one asked me where I had been – or for that matter, why I was back. I sensed that somehow they probably knew more than they let on as whispered conversations in the local post office stopped abruptly when I walked in. My lovely next door neighbours, who had kindly kept a watch on my house and the comings and goings of my (by now hopefully far away) tenant, knew part of my story, but they never pried or judged me. Similarly, the few close friends I had made in the village warmly welcomed me back and we continued to meet the local pub for its fun weekly quiz nights – the only questions asked of me being the quiz ones.

In contrast to Mellors' swift adaption to change, there was an underlying sense of resistance to change in the village generally, as is often the case in small communities. I was horrified at some of the racist reactions I witnessed when the corner shop residents of 20 years retired and a lovely, friendly family from Sri Lanka moved in. Some of these reactions were from 'good honest church-going folk' and I found the hypocrisy disturbed me and felt quite in conflict with the beauty I experienced there.

The skies were still as big as I remembered them, the sunsets still as magnificent, and I'm sure they still hadn't changed the fat in the fryer at the village fish and chip shop. This seemed only to add to the flavour of the very delicious skate and chips I often treated myself to.

As spring approached, life on dry land seemed much less eventful than it had been during my big adventure. The only drama this time was not of the nautical variety but caused by a big bird. I've never been quite sure of the difference between a rook, a jackdaw, a raven and crow – anyway, one of the avian species had built a nest in my chimney, and apparently, they do so quickly and efficiently. If builders could work that fast, the housing crisis in the UK would be over in days and *The Big Issue* would go out of business.

It disturbed me to see the little twigs and feathers dropping down into my open fireplace, wondering if a bird was shortly to follow. It disturbed me even more to think about lighting a fire, and I could not even contemplate going up a ladder to the roof to explore from the other end.

I still hadn't decided what to do when, on returning home one day, I found the decision had been made for me. As I opened the front door, the normally white walls in the sitting room were now splattered from end to end with black soot. The aforementioned 'big bird' was flapping around, and from what I could see through my hands covering my eyes, was not helping the problem. I was terrified of trapped birds so I quickly shut the door with me on the outside and went to the beach café for a coffee and to try to gather my thoughts.

An hour later, I called on my neighbour, who came in and rescued the poor bird, saying "Aw, it's only a baby!" He then very kindly attached a cowl to my chimney, which would hopefully prevent the awful event happening again.

So, as a result of my feathered house guest, I had a bit more spring cleaning to do in my house than I had anticipated. This was, however, part of a therapeutic process in clearing out my old life too.

As the Alp-like appearance created by the snow on the sand dunes slowly melted away, I was busy making a shopping list to top up my fridge (and drinks cupboard) in preparation for a family visit. All was well in my world as I prepared to welcome the changes the next phase of my life was to bring.

REFLECTIONS:
(FROM A NORFOLK VILLAGE)

 Cleaning can be therapeutic as well as a necessity.

 Scary things tend to not go away on their own – sometimes, you have to act to free yourself from your fears.

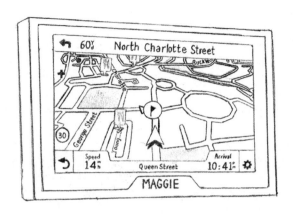

The Next
Chapter

'One day you will tell your story of how you overcame what you went through and it will be someone else's survival guide.'

Brené Brown

t was later discovered that the name Tillie means 'glorious in battle' – so as it turns out, a fitting name then for a now much stronger and happier woman who:

- ⚓ is a psychotherapist in private practice using her birth name
- ⚓ owns a watch – in fact, several – for their beauty as well as their functionality
- ⚓ overcame her fear of birds and now keeps several chickens and a cockerel
- ⚓ met her first therapist again – having worked with him in a professional collegial capacity this time
- ⚓ mainly drinks (usually homemade) gin and the occasional Shiraz (for pleasure, not to forget)
- ⚓ has adopted a dog – a Labrador cross rather than a cross Labrador – who is devoted to her and never leaves her side
- ⚓ offered Mellors a dignified death at the age of 20 – she knew it was time when he looked up at her

one morning and with his eyes he told her so – at the hands of the kindly vet who came to the house and gently and with dignity helped him on his way

⚓ has two cats, although she knows they will never replace Mellors

⚓ can sense instinctively when she is within proximity of a canal – it will always be in her blood

'Rhoda', her trusty Sat. Nav., proved not to be so trusty. Her obsession with instructing her to perform U-turns was at best irritating, and at worst dangerous. Her final words were '1,675 miles to go to reach your destination', on a short journey between Winterton and Hemsby before she expired and was relegated to her final resting place – a waste bin at Currys. 'Maggie' is 'Rhoda's' replacement – although she often provokes a minor dispute, she is certainly reliable as a woman who is 'not for turning'.

The last she heard of Argy Bargy was when she spotted he was again up for sale – the reason (rather aptly) again given as 'Divorce'.

As for the Labrador – she has never seen or heard from him again.

All names changed or removed to protect identity –
apart from the cats' and the Sat. Navs'!

About the author

The author known as Alice White has a busy psychotherapy practice run from her home in North Lincolnshire. Her passion for nature awakened from her time on a narrowboat remains. She shares her small cottage and large garden with ten chickens, a cockerel, a boisterous puppy and two cats.

This is her first book – hopefully, it won't be her last.

CONTACT DETAILS

Look out for more stories and pictures on Facebook:
AliceWhiteWriterAuthor

or contact Alice at:
AliceWhiteWriter@protonmail.com

Acknowledgements

Siân-Elin Flint-Freel, my editor, for her patience and encouragement in allowing me to 'do it my way' and her tact and sensitivity in allowing me to find out for myself when my way wouldn't work. She is always interested in hearing about new book ideas and can be contacted on sianelin.flintfreel@gmail.com

Charlotte Harker – a brilliant artist and illustrator whose work has been supported by, amongst others, Arts Council England and the Pollock Krasner Foundation. She has exhibited her work both in the UK and abroad and been shortlisted for the Jerwood Drawing Prize. Examples of her other recent work can be found at www.instagram.com/charker2001 and she can be contacted at charker2001@hotmail.com

Thanks goes to Tanya Back for her transformative typesetting work, bringing my book to life, and my good friends Susan and Caroline, who took the time to read this book and review my work so honestly.

These strong women made it unbelievably easy for me to make my dream of writing a book a reality
– thank you!

Printed in Great Britain
by Amazon